GREENE & GREENE
MASTERWORKS

TEXT BY BRUCE SMITH · PHOTOGRAPHS BY ALEXANDER VERTIKOFF

AN ARCHETYPE PRESS BOOK

CHRONICLE BOOKS · SAN FRANCISCO

Library of Congress Cataloging-in-Publication Data available.

ISBN 0-8118-1878-0

Produced by Archetype Press, Inc., Washington, D.C.
Project Director: Diane Maddex
Designer: Robert L. Wiser
Editorial Assistants: Gretchen Smith Mui and John Hovanec

Manufactured in China

Distributed in Canada by Raincoast Books
9050 Shaughnessy Street, Vancouver, B.C. V6P 6E5

10   9   8   7   6   5

Chronicle Books LLC
85 Second Street
San Francisco, CA 94105

www.chroniclebooks.com

All photographs in the book are by Alexander Vertikoff except the following: College of Environmental Design Documents Collection, University of California, Berkeley: 232; and Gamble House/ University of Southern California Greene and Greene Library: 12 both, 14, 16, 20, 21 both, 22 bottom, 24 both, 25.

Endpapers: Front, The view of the Ojai Valley from the terrace of the Pratt House in Ojai. Back, The Roman arcade in the water garden of the Fleishhacker House in Woodside.

Opening photographs: Page 1, A lantern at the entrance to the Duncan-Irwin House in Pasadena. Page 2, The Spinks House in Pasadena. Page 3, A Japanese-style lantern at the Reeve House in Long Beach. Page 5, A beamed porch overlooking the central courtyard of the Duncan-Irwin House in Pasadena. Pages 6–7, Stone arches in the Fleishhacker House arcade in Woodside. Pages 8–9, A brick fireplace against a board-and-batten wall in the Pratt House in Ojai. Pages 26–27, Metal-strapped posts at the entrance to the Thorsen House in Berkeley. Pages 50–51, The living room of the Gamble House in Pasadena.

The typography used for the titles in *Greene & Greene* was designed especially for this book by Robert L. Wiser of Archetype Press. It is adapted from hand lettering found on the ink and linen drawings of Greene and Greene in the first decade of the twentieth century, the period in which their most well known houses were designed.

The text was composed in Meyer Two, revived by David Berlow for the Font Bureau in 1994. The Hollywood film mogul Louis B. Mayer commissioned five similar Linotype fonts from 1922 to 1928 and used them in intertitles for silent films.

The ornamental initials were designed by D. Rakowski in 1991 in the style of medieval revival lettering popularized by Arts and Crafts designers to reflect their antimachine aesthetic, in which craftsmanship was exalted.

C°NTENTS

FOREWORD

The architecture and decorative arts of Charles Sumner Greene and Henry Mather Greene occupy a sacrosanct but veiled niche within the American Arts and Crafts movement. Although their work has been studied, written about, photographed, and praised by many, the mute sticks and stones of the buildings themselves have managed to conceal from general view much of the magic and charm of how they are lived in today. In Greene and Greene houses there remains a distinct and ineffable power to conjure fresh wonder and inspire adulation. Since publication of the standard books on the Greenes by Randell Makinson twenty years ago, no author until now has risen to the challenge of examining the brothers' careers through a new assessment of their best extant houses. And houses they were—not churches, nor great civic edifices, nor major public monuments. Except for the very occasional dip into commercial building design and a few modest public commissions, the Greenes focused their creative energy on meticulously shaping beautiful living spaces and furnishings that would fit a human scale and fill a human need. To put Greene and Greene into some kind of reasonable perspective is no small task, precisely because of their ability to manipulate design, craft, and materials anew for each client. This book provides that perspective with thoughtful text and visionary new photography that combine to unveil the spiritual and poetic quality running like a silken thread through the Greenes' physical objects and buildings. Other architects have enjoyed more famous careers. Many others have produced more buildings. And still others have earned more notoriety for progressive designs that advanced the discipline of architecture. But no other architects have left us with a more glowing legacy of beauty, craft, livability, and spirit than Charles and Henry Greene.

Edward R. Bosley
Director, The Gamble House
Pasadena, California

11

As the morning sun finds the entrance hall of the Gamble House, its rays cast an enchanting golden light over the main staircase. The Burmese teak is exquisitely crafted of intersecting horizontal and vertical pieces to draw the eyes as well as the feet upward.

INTRODUCTION

Seeing a Greene and Greene house for the first time may leave one amazed but unquestionably more than a little exalted. Its form is reminiscent of American bungalows, although the bungalow as we know it came afterward. Whispers of the Far East can be heard in the slight rise of the roofline and in a stone lantern on the lawn. The asymmetrical design, the preference for timbers, and the romantic play of shingles and masonry recall the Stick and Shingle Styles popular on the East Coast. Exceptional craftsmanship is apparent: the porch railing has been shaped to convey a lift in its line; the roof's rafter tails, projecting beyond the eaves, have all been rounded by hand. Touches of pure artistry make themselves known at the front door in luminous art glass and a Japanese-style lantern hanging from a bracket. Nature is clearly a part of the design. Stones and bricks and different woods seem to arise from the landscape. Covered porches wrap around the house, and pergolas extend out into the garden, obscuring the line between the natural world and the more refined universe within. Inside, the use of wood is nearly overwhelming. Mixed together are Burmese teak, Honduras mahogany, Port Orford cedar, floors of oak or maple, friezes carved in redwood. Craftsmanship reigns here as well in meticulous mortise-and-tenon joinery and corbeled beams, embraced in steel straps, that step out from the walls. Motifs are picked out in wood, plaster, and glass—in one house an owl or a crane, in another a water lily. The oval shape of a Japanese *tsuba* (sword guard) is inlaid into the furniture and reappears as the form of the dining table itself. The furniture, not surprisingly, is perfectly suited for its room and its exact location in the room. Charles Sumner Greene and Henry Mather Greene designed each piece for a particular place in a particular house for their clients. A piano against a living room wall is cased in the same mahogany used for the built-in bookcases. A rose made of vermilion wood inlaid in a dressing table is a relative of the rose in the art glass lantern on the wall next to it.

Charles Sumner Greene (top) and his brother, Henry Mather Greene (bottom), seen here about 1906, shared the same background and five decades of work, yet they were uncommonly different men. Charles was said to be under "the spell of Japan," a fascination evident at the Blacker House in Pasadena (opposite).

12

The buildings and furnishings by which we know the firm of Greene and Greene were created over a brief period of time, essentially from 1903 to 1909, all except one of them built in California. The two brothers produced great work both before and after then, but during these half dozen years, more than refining a style of architecture, they defined an aesthetic that has become so pervasive that at times it is not recognized for what it is. Sometimes mistakenly called Craftsman, sometimes absurdly labeled Japanese, their work interprets both of these two bundles of ideas yet expands, redefines, and rises far above them. 🍂 The Greenes' designs are often gathered within the Arts and Crafts movement that arose at the turn of the twentieth century; certainly their mindfulness of nature, their extraordinarily fitting use of local materials, and their reliance on skilled craftsmen all speak to the Arts and Crafts enthusiast, but they did not see their most representative work as part of this movement. Their buildings were something separate, unto themselves. Charles Greene, the older of the brothers and the primary designer for their firm, often referred to his role not as an architect but as an artist. Architecture was, as he entitled an article, "a Fine Art." 🍂 Writers of the time gathered Greene and Greene within the folds of the Arts and Crafts movement, not for the firm's later sophisticated work but for its early turn to the rustic. The simple board-and-batten Bandini House of 1903 in Pasadena was the brothers' first widely published design. Every room opened onto a central courtyard, expressing the idea of a life lived as much outside as within, a life of few possessions and modest tastes—all exemplifying the ideal of the simple life that pervaded the Arts and Crafts philosophy. Life in such a home would surely offset the harshness of the modern industrial age. 🍂 Early on Charles and the younger Henry were exposed to both the reality of industrialization and the ideal of simplicity. Born to city life, Charles in 1868 and Henry in 1870, they spent their youth in the mercantile port of Cincinnati, moving when Charles was five and Henry four to a rapidly urbanizing St. Louis. Their father, Thomas Sumner Greene, started out as a bookkeeper but later studied homeopathic medicine to become a doctor specializing in catarrh, a disease of the nose and throat. Both he and the boys' mother, Lelia Mather Greene, came from old New England families: the Revolutionary War Major-General Nathanael Greene on the father's side and Cotton Mather on the mother's. The brothers escaped the city to spend summers on their grandfather Mather's farm in West Virginia. The memoirs of Henry Greene's son Henry Dart Greene describe how "clad only in shirts and overalls, the boys helped their grandfather with light farm chores, but more memorably fished, swam, read and enjoyed the outdoors to their hearts content." It was an old-fashioned farm, "self-reliant and self-sufficient," where the Greene boys would have seen in those formative years everything from blacksmithing to carpentry, from growing food to making soap. 🍂 A love of the pastoral is obvious in the refined simplicity incorporated into all of their houses, from small ones designed throughout their careers to their most sophisticated residences from the years 1905–11. Simple, unpainted wood paneling was sufficient for the interior walls, although the wood they chose was often rare. Where not paneled in wood, walls would be plastered and covered in canvas, then painted with restful earth tones. For a slight decorative touch, Charles might apply a Japanesque motif of branches and flowers across a plaster-and-canvas–covered frieze panel.

15

Across from Charles Greene's own home on Arroyo Terrrace in Pasadena, massive twisting oaks shaded the gentle California landscape. Charles, who always wanted to be an artist, took this photograph himself. He named his house Oakholm and used the image of the oak in many designs over the years, including the art glass doors for the Gamble House, built immediately above this country road.

Jennie Reeve's 1904 house in Long Beach was one of the earliest Greene and Greene residences in which Charles expressed his infatuation with Asian designs. Clearly Japanesque in style, the lantern in the cozy inglenook (above) was among the brothers' first lighting fixtures. At the Blacker House of 1907 (opposite), corbeled redwood posts with metal straps gracefully allude to historic Japanese temples.

UNDER THE ASIAN INFLUENCE

The Far East was always an element in the Greenes' work. They drew from both China and Japan, although their idealized vision of Japan was more of an influence. The brothers were first exposed to Japanese art and culture during their university years in Boston, where they attended the Massachusetts Institute of Technology. Lectures on this newly opened Asian country were often presented in the city; the Museum of Fine Arts held the country's major collection of Japanese pottery and art along with special exhibitions of crafts and woodblock prints. The pair later viewed examples of Japanese architecture and crafts at international expositions, and Charles especially would later haunt shops in Los Angeles and San Francisco that sold oriental curios and furniture, purchasing pieces for himself and clients. The Asian influence was first openly expressed in the interiors of the Greenes' Culbertson House of 1902 in Pasadena, becoming more overt in the Japanesque lighting for the Reeve House of 1904 in Long Beach, and then, following Charles's visit to the Japanese exhibits at the 1904 Louisiana Purchase Exposition in St. Louis, guiding the entire design that year for the Long Beach home of Jennie Reeve's friend Adelaide Tichenor. From then on it was rare not to find Far Eastern elements in their work. From Chinese furniture came the "cloud lift" (a slight elevation in a horizontal line), used as a motif across door transoms, in chair rails, for lanterns, and on benches in inglenooks; it became one of their signature features. Corbeled bracing on their porches brings to mind Japanese temples. The Greenes' orientalism was most exquisite in their largest commissions, notably the home designed for Robert and Nellie Blacker in 1907. The lily pond and pergola, the great lantern hanging at the end of the porte cochere, the terrace's timber joinery supported by steel straps, and the wood staircase all evoke a vision of Japan that was uniquely the Greenes'.

s surely as the brothers' Far Eastern vision orig-inated in Boston, so did their use of materials and the arrangement of their interiors. The Greenes were probably influenced less by the Beaux Arts training they received at MIT and more by their apprenticeships with Boston architecture firms. After a special two-year certificate program in architecture at MIT, Charles and Henry worked with architects who had trained under the great architect Henry Hobson Richardson. Here they would have become familiar with the Shingle Style—commodious shingle-clad buildings then popular in the East—and de-signs for houses that grew out of central living halls, whose rooms flowed one into another yet had private window seats in bay windows or cozy inglenooks around a fireplace, their stairways rising grandly from spacious entries. They would also have seen materials, whether brick or wood paneling, stone or tile, used in a way that was honest to the material itself, without the need for added surface ornamentation. All of these became elements in the Greenes' vocabulary.

Although Charles and Henry no doubt encountered skilled craftsmen in Boston, craftsmanship was something in which they had already been trained. For high school their father had enrolled his sons in the new Manual Training School of Washington University in St. Louis, the country's first school of its kind. During the three-year course, the boys spent half of each day on academic subjects, the other half on drawing lessons and in the shop learning car-pentry, metalworking, and similar trades. This training served Charles and Henry well in their architectural prac-tice. Not only were they able to guide artisans by example, the brothers were also knowledgeable enough about the craft process to grant artisans the freedom to carry out their own work. During the Greenes' most fruitful years, they gathered around them a number of master crafts-men—especially Emil Lange, the art glass artist; Peter Hall, who served as contractor for most of their work after 1905; and his brother John Hall, who oversaw the mill shop where the Greenes' furniture was constructed.

From one room to another, spaces in the Bolton House (above) flow freely as they do in Shingle Style houses along the East Coast. The Greenes' extraordinary craftsmanship, however, sets it apart. For Mary Gamble's desk in her bedroom (opposite), a pattern was inlaid from a favorite Rookwood vase she brought from Cincinnati—an exemplary example of the collaboration between the brothers Greene and Hall.

20

alifornia's influence on the Greenes was powerful. They arrived in Pasadena in the fall of 1893 to join their parents, who had moved there just a year earlier. A freshness in the land prevailed then, a spirit and energy that are now long gone. Only recently founded, Pasadena was a sophisticated town, one that for a decade before the Greenes' arrival had been the state's preeminent resort for tourists from the East. "California, with its climate, so wonderful in its possibility, is only beginning to be dreamed of . . . ," Charles wrote. The area provided a perfect mixture of eastern erudition and a freedom from social and class restraints that allowed the Greenes to take their architecture in directions inconceivable in the traditional East. California also provided them with clients who could afford the workmanship and artistry of their designs. ❧ Charles was twenty-five years old, Henry just short of twenty-four when they opened their architecture office with high ambitions in January 1894, just a few months after coming west. Within three years they had moved to larger quarters in one of the best located buildings in Pasadena, one they themselves had designed. In 1901 the *Los Angeles Builder and Contractor* announced: "Greene and Greene have opened a branch office in Los Angeles." Clients willing, their commissions involved not just house designs but also furniture, carpets, lighting, art glass, and landscaping. The brothers exerted total control over their houses. ❧ Henry Greene's son remembers that his Uncle Charles "by nature was an artist and designer," whereas his father "excelled in the construction and 'getting things done' categories." Their offices at the firm reflected this. The floor of Charles's office was covered with oriental carpets. A cabinet against one wall held art objects and books on art and architecture. Henry's office, in contrast, was the image of practicality and productivity, with drawing boards, filing cabinets, and shelves that held product catalogues. The pattern had been set quickly: Henry ran the office. Charles met with clients and, often from the upstairs studio in his home, would create the designs and turn over his sketches to the draftsmen. Less than 20 percent of Greene and Greene's work was outside the Pasadena area, even though they ventured as far north as Vancouver, British Columbia. 🌿 By 1899 Henry was married to Emeline Augusta Dart, who boarded in his aunt's home, which the Greenes had designed. Two years later, Charles married Alice Gordon White, an English woman who resided less than a block from where he was living with his parents. Needing rest from the firm's intense work in 1909, Charles took his family for a nine-month stay in England while Henry managed Greene and Greene by himself. 🌿 When Charles returned, he gradually began withdrawing from their practice. He wrote a romantic novel about a young architect, kidnapped to an island in the South Pacific to design a house for a beautiful woman. In 1916 he retreated north to the artistic community of Carmel. Henry continued practicing architecture, at first involving Charles at a distance, but by 1922 the two brothers had stopped using the name Greene and Greene. Henry worked on alone; Charles did some architecture but more and more devoted himself to his artistic and spiritual pursuits.

Charles, photographed about 1900 with his future wife, Alice, during a picnic in the Arroyo Seco (opposite), was always more the artist, whereas Henry, seen at his drafting table (right top), ably ran the firm of Greene and Greene. By balancing their different temperaments, the brothers were able to reach the heights of design found in this table and lamp for the Blacker House (right bottom).

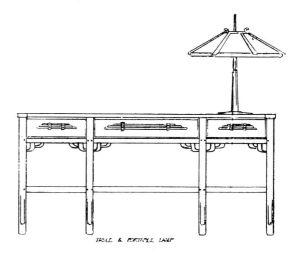

TABLE & PORTABLE LAMP

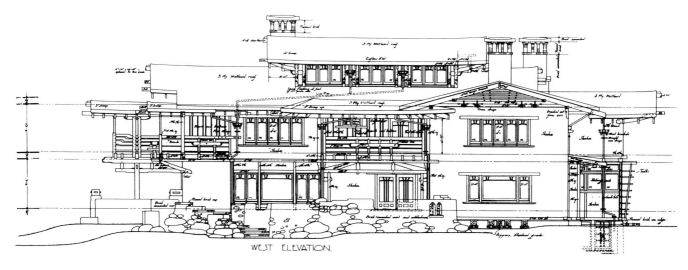

WEST ELEVATION.

It is easy, but too simplistic, to classify Charles as the artist and Henry as the businessman. They may have begun in this manner, but by the end of their careers each had excelled architecturally in his own way. For Charles there was always a tension between art and architecture. By nature he was an artist; by economic necessity—to satisfy his parents' aspirations—both he and Henry had been directed to architecture by their father. ❧ Charles once had to defend to a client his use of rafters that projected beyond the roofline. It was simple and basic to him: "The reason why the beams project from the gables is because they cast such beautiful shadows on the sides of the house in this bright atmosphere." Beauty was what mattered, carefully calculated and exquisitely crafted. Years later, in a letter to a different client, Charles wrote to justify the expense of constructing a stone wall: "It is too much to expect that anyone may see the excellence of this kind of thing in a few days. The work itself took months to execute and the best years of my life went to develop this style.... Into your busy life I have sought to bring what lay in my power of the best that I could do for Art and for you." ❧ In May 1947, two cousins came to meet the seventy-seven-year-old Henry so that he could show them around Pasadena, pointing out with pride the work he had done so many years before. Without a home of his own, he was living with a son's family in Altadena. By then Greene and Greene's work was virtually forgotten. The little entourage went to the Williams House of 1915 and the Crow-Crocker House of 1909, both products of Henry's hand alone, and to the grand Robinson House of 1905. There, the new owner "was so flattered by our enjoyment," one of the cousins wrote to Charles in Carmel, "that he took us all over the house and listened to Hal with the keenest attention." And, she told Charles, "We saw your home and admired your view...."

23

Sheltered from the California sunshine by gabled roofs and gently lifted above the terrain by walls of arroyo stone and clinker brick, the Gamble House exemplifies the best of the work of Charles and Henry Greene. Transitions between outside and inside are easy and natural. Banks of windows coax nature indoors, while sleeping porches allowed the family to savor the healthful night air. On the terrace, shade beckons beneath overhangs built for that purpose.

24

any years earlier Charles had conducted a similar tour, not for family but for the noted English Arts and Crafts architect and designer C. R. Ashbee. It was 1909, and the Greenes were at the height of their careers. At the brothers' furniture workshop "they were making without exception the best and most characteristic furniture I have seen in this country. There were beautiful cabinets and chairs of [mahogany] and lignum-vitae, exquisite doweling and pegging, and in all a supreme feeling for the material, quite up to the best of our English craftsmanship. . . . " From here they went to Arroyo Terrace, where Charles's own 1901 home stood, alongside an enclave of other Greene and Greene designs built from 1903 to 1907. Most likely they stopped to

inspect the Gamble House, just being finished on Westmoreland Place. Charles then took his visitor to tea with Mrs. James A. Garfield, widow of the assassinated president. The Englishman fingered the wood paneling and watched as "a glorious sunset lit the snow on the mountains to rose red." Her 1904 house, of course, was another Greene and Greene design. Taking his leave, Ashbee noted in his journal: "I think C. Sumner Greene's work beautiful; among the best there is in this country. Like [Frank] Lloyd Wright the spell of Japan is on him, he feels the beauty and makes magic out of the horizontal line, but there is in his work more tenderness, more subtlety, more self effacement than in Wright's work. It is more refined and has more repose."

TRANSCENDENT ARCHITECTURE

Today the houses designed by Charles and Henry Greene are appreciated for far different reasons than when they were built. Then, despite all the allusions to the past, they were extraordinarily modern, with up-to-date conveniences and the latest appliances. They provided an architectural alternative to the staid Colonial Revival and neoclassical styles popular in the early years of the twentieth century. They sated the desire for something romantic and exotic in a world growing more mundane. The heights of craftsmanship that the Greenes achieved spoke at the time merely of quality and expense, not of the lost past as it does now. But the work of the Greenes cannot be viewed simply as a West Coast deviant of proper East Coast architecture—in truth, it is some of the finest, most subtly beautiful architecture ever designed and built anywhere. A transformation takes place when one enters a Greene and Greene house. Left behind is information-age technology; in its stead is a time when all workmanship was done well, when all edges were rounded and all joints pegged and tenoned; a space where a synthesis has been reached between East and West, between the excitement and romance of the exotic and the comfort and warmth of the home; a place in which nature has become a part of life rather than an element to be struggled against. There is more than a mastery of craftsmanship here. In Greene and Greene's houses there is a refined artistic vision, one that transcends architecture and enters the realm of art.

Beginning in 1904 Henry and his family shared the home of his mother-in-law, Charlotte Whitridge (opposite top). Designed by Greene and Greene, it was demolished in 1968. The same fate threatens the chaletlike residence of President James A. Garfield's widow (opposite bottom). Charles and Henry (right), photographed in the late 1940s, were honored by the American Institute of Architects in 1952 as "formulators of a new and native architecture."

THE GREENE & GREENE STYLE

"THE IDEA WAS TO ELIMINATE EVERY-
THING UNNECESSARY, TO MAKE THE
WHOLE AS DIRECT AND SIMPLE AS POS-
SIBLE, BUT ALWAYS WITH THE BEAUTIFUL
IN MIND AS THE FIRST GOAL · · · · "

HENRY GREENE, 1912

Rare are the architects like Greene and Greene who are able to transcend mere competence, to create in a structure a higher level of experience. Charles Greene suggested in 1908 that "there are three great things the prospective builder should know by heart." First, he said, was that "good work costs much more than poor imitation or factory product." The designs of Greene and Greene, while alluding to much—from the Japanese temple to the Spanish hacienda, from shingled houses of the eastern seaboard to rustic cabins in the mountains—were never a poor imitation of anything. "No house however expensive," Charles noted as his second reason, "can be a success unless you, the owners, give the matter time and thought enough to know what you want it for." Utility and function always mattered to the Greenes. Because California summers were so warm, their houses were cross ventilated and the roofs had broad overhangs. Windows looked out naturally onto vistas, and doors led easily to terraces or a garden. The most important item on Charles's list, he dictated, was that "you must employ some one who is broad enough to understand and sympathize with you and your needs and yet has the ability to put them into shape from the artist's point of view." ✵ The work of Charles and Henry Greene comprises a number of readily identifiable elements: rafter tails that project outward to cast shadows on the walls, broad porches and terraces with structural timberwork reminiscent of Japan, a roughness in clinker bricks against smooth fieldstones, shingled walls, earth-toned colors, a poetic use of the Chinese "cloud lift" motif. But only when it is all put together, "from the artist's point of view," do these features become more than disparate elements and achieve the transcendent experience of a Greene and Greene design.

Casa Barranca, the Pratt family's name for its house in Ojai, is set so naturally into the landscape that it seems to have become part of it. Rafters ease beyond the roofline to paint the "beautiful shadows" beloved by the artist in Charles Greene. The signature of Greene and Greene can be found in every feature and material.

EXTERIORS

ach stylistic element of a Greene and Greene house has its own reason for being. The roofline's broad, low pitch, its eaves projecting far beyond the walls, helps cool the interior from the California sun. Sleeping porches, with their board-and-batten paneling and wall lanterns, provide outdoor rooms for hot summer nights. The porches' Japanesque post-and-beam timbering actually lends structural support. Often, however, the reason behind a feature is purely allusive: small-paned leaded glass windows that recall the Middle Ages, massive round stone chimneys that tie a building to the land, door frames designed in the shape of a Japanese *torii* (temple entrance) to cast an oriental spirit about the house.

A Greene and Greene house can be most easily identified by expressive timber framing, coupled with shingles like late-nineteenth-century architecture in the East. Horizontal bands of redwood between the shingles outside delineate interior floors. Repeated rafter tails across the length of an eave form playful patterns juxtaposed with matchstick-like sleeping porches extending out over terraces. Many houses have generous porte cocheres constructed of redwood post-and-beam timbers with stones or brickwork. In the larger houses rooflines are never simple. The twin gables of the Blacker House in Pasadena, for example, are amplified by a large porte cochere and a balconied terrace. Together all the elements signal a unity of vision.

The Gamble House (opposite) was outfitted with sleeping porches off each of the family bedrooms. Rough woven matting appropriate for the outside covers the floors, but the walls are finished in board and batten—announcing that these upstairs porches, while outside, are meant to be treated as part of the inside of the house. The strongly gabled front of the Spinks House (above) is marked by studied rows of shingles, relieved by an inset porch, bands of redwood timbers, and windows that Greene and Greene placed in exactly the right spots.

Undulating bricks embedded with arroyo stones at the Duncan-Irwin House (above left) seem to have been stacked by nature rather than at the direction of the architects. At a distance, the white Gunite walls of the Culbertson Sisters House (above right) look smooth, but up close it is obvious that the hands of a workman have shaped them. The chimney designed for the Cole House (opposite), a neighbor of the Gamble House, creates a smooth transition from the ground upward into the sky—a masterful arrangement of local arroyo stones.

MATERIALS

The first houses the Greenes designed were painted outside, but it was not long until they were working with stucco and half-timber framing, coverings of shingles, and assertive redwood construction. Their rustic designs with board-and-batten interior and exterior walls and massive stone fireplaces were the first to be published, followed soon by their large shingle-covered houses. What was never conveyed in those days before color printing was the soft pine forest—green hue achieved on the shingles by dipping in a creosote stain. Or the intensity of dark red clinker brick placed against a hand-rounded, soft brown—stained redwood porch post. Although large, the Greene houses always seem to cling to the earth—stone walls are worked in with clinker brick; porch steps are more refined pressed brick, while the porch itself is terra-cotta tile. Each material integrates the house to its surroundings and leads to the next, from coarseness outside to sublimity inside.

ENTRANCES

arely in a Greene and Greene house is there an abrupt division between inside and out. One enters by transitions, in stages. Brick steps may lead up from the garden to a porch. Shelter comes from a gabled overhang or a sleeping porch that extends from above—one is covered but still able to feel the breeze. The pattern in the door's art glass evokes the natural world being left behind. 🦋 Stepping inside, one still does not feel totally enclosed; across the entrance hall are doorways framing a vista of gardens beyond. On hot days, the side doors bracketing the front entrance are left open, inviting the air to circulate. For more urban houses, the Greenes designed doors with less glass, but those set back from the street often have grand art glass designs. In the countryside, clear glass in simple doors allows the natural world to become part of the interior world.

34

Designed in the formal English manner, the front entrance of the Ware House (above) is protected by the overhang of the shingled second story. At the Blacker House (right), a protective porte cochere supported by massive posts and beams and lighted by Japanesque lanterns guides visitors to the impressive front door.

STAIRCASES

More than other architects of their time, the Greenes allowed stairways to arise sculpturally within entries, to define and clarify the hall space. In the Pasadena houses for the Blacker and Gamble families, the staircases rise grandly and turn back over the front door, providing a canopy above the entry—a place where visitors can pause to take a breath while absorbing the hall's beauty. Although some say that the great Romanesque architect Henry Hobson Richardson of Boston influenced their stairway designs, the brothers were able to move beyond their East Coast training, allowing motifs to emerge from negative space in banister slats or providing a gentle reminder of Japan, as in the graceful stepped handrail of the Gamble House. Even in the less grandiose houses, stairways were still carefully crafted transitions between floors. A skylight or windows were placed to light the landings. Bottom steps are spread wide, easing the passage downstairs, while articulated risers and angled Japanesque panels in the banister lead one gracefully upward.

An assertive newel post in the main stairway of the Blacker House (opposite) recalls Japanese temple designs while it supports the second floor with a corbeled, or stepped, brace. At the same time, it provides a fine place to hang a lantern. Steps turn and pour down the Van Rossem–Neill House staircase (above left) to offer a wide, sturdy platform at the bottom. Even a simple, narrow stair in Charles Greene's own home (above right) was planned and finished with care, pulling climbers up higher and higher in the four-level residence.

FURNISHINGS

he work of the Greenes epitomizes the concept that the architect not only should be the designer of the exterior structure and interior detailing but also should be allowed total control of the environment within. From the first pieces of furniture the Greenes designed, strongly influenced by Gustav Stickley's Craftsman style, to their more refined pieces with designs drawn from Chinese household furniture, their furniture was intended as part of a room's composition—to be placed in a particular room in a particular spot. They worked with a variety of woods, including Honduras mahogany, teak, ash, maple, and oak, and often inlaid designs using fruitwoods, ebony, oak, copper, silver, brass, and abalone shell. In addition to furniture, they designed picture frames, carpets, lighting fixtures, jewelry boxes, curtains, clocks, andirons, and fire screens, all custom designed for each client. ✿ Many, although not all, of the designs were by Charles, but Henry's influence can be seen at times—for example, in the ingenious way the Gamble House dining table can be extended to take additional leaves. Either brother's designs were made more successful because of the relationship established with the master craftsmen Peter and John Hall. From 1905 on, the Hall brothers, working hand-in-hand with Charles, oversaw the artisans who produced the varied furnishings with which the Greenes filled their houses.

Greene and Greene had Peter and John Hall create a complete suite of furniture for the dining room of the Thorsen House in Berkeley using both mahogany and ebony. The inlaid floral pattern of oak, fruitwoods, and abalone shell in the sideboard matches inlays on the table's surface and on the backs of the dining chairs.

JOINERY

Charles and Henry Greene had a fascination with where things meet. Whether on furniture or in interior details, rarely do two pieces come together on the same level. Although screws are used to construct a rocking chair, visible signs send another message: the back rail is joined to the side bars by splines, thin pieces of ebony inserted into grooves to join the two pieces, which are then pegged in a pattern that has been called "dancing." Always, the edges and the pegs are rounded; never is there the abruptness of a sharp edge. The Greenes' early work recalls the articulated joinery of Stickley's Craftsman furniture, with exposed mortise-and-tenon joints and pegs that protrude. Quickly the Greenes allowed in more of the Orient—the forms became rounded, softer, the woods more rare. Metal straps held together beams, with two straps encircling the rounded pieces of lumber, which were then joined by metal wedges. These wedge shapes are reminiscent of scarf joints found in the shipbuilder's vocabulary, in Chinese furniture design, and in Japanese temple construction. The Greenes often used these scarf joints structurally but even more so as a design element in their interiors, providing motion to a room's design, the arrow pattern of the joint directing one's eyes around the space.

Finger-jointed risers and a pegged mortise-and-tenon banister in Charles Greene's own home (left) demonstrate his concern with how elements are put together. In the Gamble House's intricately constructed staircase, which rises up over the front entry (opposite), each end is rounded, each corner is smoothed.

LIGHTING

Greene and Greene lighting was always about more than just light. A lantern softly lit on a terrace casts a spell over an evening. A copper hood tells of things Japanese. A stained glass chandelier over a dining table sends light upward to see by and downward to shed a golden hue. In the Blacker House living room, the six-sided lanterns display art glass patterns of lilies copied from the pond outside, then direct the bare light upward to reflect off the ceiling's molded lilies and ripples of water covered in gold leaf. Some of their lighting was truly innovative. The Robinson House's dining room chandelier could easily be lowered or raised by a system of weights. For the Thorsen House living room, Charles recessed the lighting into the ceiling. For the poor-sighted Mary Ware, Henry developed indirect lighting for the living room to spare her any glare from the new electric light bulbs. More than merely providing illumination, Greene and Greene lighting continued the all-important elements of craftsmanship, motif, and romantic allusion.

43

Diners at the Pratt House (opposite) are bathed in soft light from an elegantly elongated chandelier of leaded iridescent glass, its panels fitted into a mahogany frame. A Gamble House fixture (left) casts a strong light upward to reflect off the ceiling as well as a gentle colored light downward to give warmth to the living room.

ART GLASS

agic is cast by light filtered through colored glass into a room of dark wood. By waving this magic wand, the Greenes exerted incredible control over their interiors. Following their early, fairly straightforward stained glass in the houses for Jennie Reeve and Adelaide Tichenor, they soon were designing intricate, abstract work. The clear glass and leaded came in James Culbertson's house formed an Art Nouveau pattern that could have been rising streams of smoke. At the height of their work, their large residences of 1905–9, came masterful exercises in integrating colored light with motif, functionality with artistry. ❦ Taken individually, each element of each art glass panel becomes an abstraction, a pattern of shape and color. But when the entire window or door is experienced as a whole, the genius of the design takes shape. Allusions to the world at hand can be seen: a trailing rose pattern when a rose bush grows just beyond, a stepped pattern in soft browns for a window opening onto a stairway. ❦ The Greenes achieved a richness of color in their glasswork without resorting to stains by building up naturally colored glass in layers, at times so high the effect was three-dimensional. As the hour changes in a house, as lights are turned on and off and the sun enters from different angles, the colors evolve, and the patterns often seem to as well.

44

The Culbertson House's oak-patterned art glass door—now set into a wall of plate glass (right)—was spared when the house was altered. Awaiting all who ascend the Blacker House's main staircase is a magnificent window of colored glass (opposite). Grape vines undulate in wood-framed panels above a trellis of bamboo.

An inviting brick fireplace in the Pratt family's country retreat in Ojai (above) bears geometric patterns that contrast with the simple walls. Now restored with original Grueby tiles, the fireside inglenook in the Bolton House (right) is typical of Greene and Greene designs intended to attract residents to the heart of their home.

FIREPLACES

At a time when technological advances rendered the fireplace superfluous, the Greenes, like other architects of the Arts and Crafts era, made them central to their designs—in fact, the houses were built around them. In front of the fireplace, benches would be placed and bookshelves built in, reminding the home-owners that this was a place to gather, to sit in comfort. Fireplaces became part of the interior design through the Greenes' careful choice of materials and motifs. From pressed-brick fronts to cobblestone, from tiles inlaid with opaque glass to clinker brick, each hearth was designed individually for each room. Not overlooked usually were the andirons and fire screens and occasionally the hearthside tools.

GARDENS

ust as the Greenes wielded control over interiors, they also concerned themselves with how a house was placed within the landscape. Great care was taken to site their houses around existing trees, so that they become an integral part of the structure. A clinker-brick wall at the property's edge ties the cultivated landscape of a garden to the wilder landscape beyond. A rounded-stone path seemingly created by nature shows the way to a side entrance. Pergolas, trellised gateways, and benches and seats connect the life of the house to the world outside. Ponds provide coolness in the warm summer air. Several times the Greenes were given an opportunity to do more than just place a house in an existing landscape. In 1911 the Culbertson sisters of Pasadena had them design a garden in the Italianate style, and then in the late 1920s Charles on his own designed for the Fleishhackers a water garden on their estate in Woodside. In all their work, they treated the exterior setting with the same respect accorded to the house itself.

At the Fleishhacker family estate in Woodside (opposite), rough stone steps flanked by brick urns lead from the formal gardens of the main house to the Roman pond and water garden below. There, a rustic stone arcade crowns Charles Greene's most spectacular landscape design. Water also refreshes the Gamble House (above), where a serpentine curve in the wall of clinker brick and stone on the back terrace forms a naturalistic barrier for the lily pond. With goldfish swimming under the lilies, more than a hint of Japan was alluded to here.

LIVING THE ARTS & CRAFTS LIFE

"... WHEN ONE APPROACHES SUCH A HOUSE IT MUST NOT OBTRUDE ITSELF UPON ONE'S SIGHT, BUT RATHER FIT INTO THE THINGS ABOUT IT .... GOOD THINGS ARE NOT ALWAYS SEEN AT ONCE, BUT THEY DO NOT NEED AD-VERTISING WHEN THEY ARE FOUND."

CHARLES GREENE, 1905

CHARLES GREENE HOUSE

When Charles Greene began building his own home in Pasadena in 1901, a large family was probably far from his mind. Alice White, whom he married that February, had just finished caring for her father up until his recent death, and she had already begun to fill a similar role for her high-strung, nervous-tempered, artistic husband. In fact, their wedding date was moved forward two weeks when Charles became ill and Alice was needed to move into his rental home to take care of him. Charles had been raised in a small family with just one brother, so it is likely that neither Charles nor Alice spent their time daydreaming about having more than one or two children—although they ended up with five. For their honeymoon, the couple crossed the Atlantic to England, Alice's birthplace, and then proceeded on to the Continent. They toured for several months and returned late in the summer to take up their new married life in Pasadena. On their way back across the country they stopped at the Pan-American Exposition in Buffalo to see some photographs of work by the relatively new firm of Greene and Greene. Visiting the exposition exposed Charles to the latest achievements of the American Arts and Crafts movement. There Gustav Stickley introduced to the public his new line of United Craftsman furniture. Joseph P. McHugh and Company was just adding the name "Mission" to the Arts and Crafts vocabulary with the Mission-style furniture it was exhibiting there for the first time. Louis Comfort Tiffany, the Grueby Faience Company, Rookwood Pottery from Charles's hometown of Cincinnati, Newcomb Pottery, the furniture of Charles Rohlfs, and the fashionable new look of the hand-hammered silver work of Gorham Manufacturing—all were on display in Buffalo. Charles could hardly have missed the announcements of Stickley's forthcoming magazine, *The Craftsman*, to be published later that year. The England that Charles saw was still architecturally under the influence of Richard Norman Shaw and the Queen Anne revival movement, levened by a cadre of Arts and Crafts architects such as C. F. A. Voysey, William Lethaby, and Edwin Lutyens. He would have been exposed to an active yet more conservative Arts and Crafts movement than the one on display in Buffalo. English proponents looked further backwards than their American cousins, to the medieval rather than the colonial, and had taken up with a passion the inglenook, the massive fireplace, leaded glass windows, window seats, hipped gables, half-timbered second stories, and decorative brick chimneys, all building to a picturesque irregularity that must have been a breath of fresh air after the rigid Beaux Arts architectural training the Greenes went through at MIT.

Set above the street by a wall of clinker brick and arroyo stone, Charles Greene's own home started as a simple, one-story structure of shingle and stucco. But by the time he moved to Carmel in 1916, it had evolved into six bedrooms and three bathrooms, all rising up four levels. Living room windows in an octagonal bay look west out over the arroyo. Playful rooflines made good climbing for the children.

akholm, as Charles called his home, reflected this sense of freedom. His marriage in 1901, at the age of thirty-three, provided the funds he needed (Alice's inheritance) to purchase a prime piece of Pasadena property overlooking the arroyo and to build a comfortable house, from which he was to do much of his design work. "From its high position above the street one has one of the finest views of the arroyo and mountains," Charles noted. 🌰 It began as a small, two-bedroom house with more fireplaces than bathrooms (one), placed on a turn in the street named Arroyo Terrace. Charles observed a few years later that "Arroyo Terrace is not a straight street but is an irregular curve from one end to the other, thus no house can be set at a right angle to the street." Raised above it beyond a wall of natural rocks built in with bricks, the site permitted "the needed privacy to those who would enjoy the view from out of doors" and also protected it "from the dust of street traffic." To accommodate the street as it bends around the house, Charles created a design that faces outward at all angles. 🌰 Looking out the windows of the living room, the Greenes could see toward the west; standing at the sink in the kitchen, the view was northward to the mountains. Between the two rooms was Charles's studio, built as a two-level octagonal room; the second level, accessible only by a ladder, featured an eight-sided walkway forming a library. From his studio windows both the mountains and the arroyo filled Charles's view. 🌰 Later, as part of his ongoing additions and alterations for the Greenes' expanding family, Charles added a complete second level. The octagonal second-story area then became his workroom, and the downstairs studio evolved into a den. In his aerie studio, his drawing table was positioned, and the windows designed accordingly, to give him views not only of both directions along the street but also of the mountains in the background. There nature's colors and textures stimulated him to create incomparable works of art over the next fifteen years.

55

Board-and-batten wall paneling, plain yet well-considered construction in the stairway, and simple redwood doors with sliding latches illustrate the straightforward craftsmanship that underlay Charles's art. Early on this room was his "at home" architecture studio, although when the house was expanded it became his den.

Charles was constantly experimenting with ideas and designs that made their way into his larger masterworks. Remaining in the house are door latches that can be locked by dropping a simple lever (top left), joinery carefully fitted together with all the surfaces rounded (top right), pieces of Grueby tile inset into stucco (above left), and bronze and steel used as a decorative floral inlay in a fireplace header (above right). The main fireplace (opposite) steps up to the stucco ceiling, whose arched angles lend a formality absent in other rooms.

CULBERTSON HOUSE

ike Charles Greene, James Culbertson bought a piece of land, a wheat field, on the edge of the arroyo, just yards from where Charles was already building his own home and studio. Culbertson was one of the wealthy outsiders, an investor in Michigan lumber who wintered in Pasadena, staying at a downtown hotel just a block from the office of Greene and Greene, who became his architects. ❧ Moving from the Hotel Green to his new Greene house in 1902, Culbertson found a respectable two-story structure, the second level finished with shingles and timber, the first in a lighter-colored stucco. It was a classic English Tudor design, something the Greenes would have been familiar with from their East Coast days and Charles's honeymoon visit to England the year before. ❧ Charles chose to furnish the house with Stickley furniture as well as Rookwood pottery and Tiffany accessories, all of which he would have seen at the 1901 Buffalo exposition. *Good Housekeeping* in 1906 observed that "the furniture and woodwork of [the living room] give a feeling of having been designed simultaneously, or one with the other continually in mind." Yet the interior woodwork of the Greenes' designs was more refined than the straightforward construction of Stickley's chairs and tables. Some early Japanese influence seems visible in the ceiling trim and chimney breast. ❧ How the Greenes became introduced to things Japanese is not certain. During their formative years in Boston as students and then as young working men, the city was replete with the new aesthetic now called *Japonisme*. Edward Morse, Ernest Fenollosa, and other Japanophiles lectured and wrote during the brothers' years in Boston, and the Museum of Fine Arts was developing its major collection of Japanese art objects. Charles's own copy of Morse's *Japanese Homes and Their Surroundings* (1886), then the primary resource on Japanese domestic architecture, was inscribed by him in 1902, the year in which the Greenes designed the Culbertson House.

59

The house began life as an English Tudor, but a remodeling in 1953 drastically altered its outward appearance: the entire second story was removed and much of the first floor was converted to suit a more contemporary lifestyle. Fortunately, key features of the original Greene and Greene design were saved and remain today.

ames Culbertson died in 1915. His wife lived until 1950 but died without children to leave the house to. The nephew who inherited it died the same year of the bequest; his remarried widow believed the house was too large, the kitchen too small and dark. She wanted to tear it down and start again from scratch on this piece of prime Pasadena property. Rather than demolish the house, the couple's architect, Whitney Smith, persuaded his clients to preserve elements of the Greenes' design within their new house. The entire exposed-timber second story was removed, the living room was converted into a master bedroom, and what had been the library was greatly enlarged and changed into a living room with large expanses of windows overlooking the new deck and pool as well as the arroyo. 🍂 Preserved from the old house was the massive front door, now set into a new glassed front entrance that incorporates the original leaded glass panels. Also saved was much of the dining room, including the light fixture, the wood paneling, and Charles's whimsical carving of flying birds in the ceiling panels of the bay window overlooking the front lawn. The small, circular pergola that once opened off the living room was spared as part of a back terrace facing the arroyo and today serves as an adjunct to the master bedroom. 🍃 Both Charles and Henry were still living when the house was so drastically altered, Henry with his son in Altadena and Charles in his studio in Carmel. One can only wonder whether they would rather have seen something totally new erected or whether they would have appreciated the preservation of elements of their early work in the essentially new structure. Many other Greene and Greene houses have been brashly pulled down; at least here we can be thankful that care and concern were taken with the spirit of their design.

Outdoor living spaces were integral to the work of the Greenes. Sitting under the pergola overlooking the arroyo (right) provides the same pleasure today as it did back in 1902. A trellis-covered bench (pages 62–63), designed as part of a 1906 garage addition, creates a quiet place from which to contemplate the gardens.

60

64

A glimpse of the Culbertson House as it once was can be seen in the dining room, with its mahogany and iridescent glass chandelier (above) and the original bay window of leaded glass (right). A flock of Charles's playful birds in flight spans the ceiling over the bay. The remodeling also spared the wood paneling in the room.

DARLING HOUSE

he first international exposure for the Greenes came in the biannual *Academy Architecture and Architectural Review*, published in London in 1903. Exterior and interior drawings as well as floor plans showed off their house for Mary Reeve Darling, built in Claremont that same year. Why was this house chosen to represent their work at this early stage in their careers? Possibly because it was the first Greene and Greene commission outside Pasadena. But it was also a house of which Charles was proud. His bold drawings were done after the house was built or under way and represented surprisingly accurately how the house looked then and now. Surrounded by trees today, the broad gambrel roof gives this small house a real presence on its street corner. Low, beamed ceilings inside produce comfortable, homey rooms that would be close to constraining boxes save for the openness between the rooms and the window seats and alcove. Kenneth Darling, Mary's son, has reminisced that "when the sliding doors were thrown aside, the entire length of the house could be converted virtually into a single room." Kenneth called the study, one of the two main rooms, "my own private sanctum for pursuits scholastic." He also remembered with special fondness "evenings spent in intimate converse with house guests around the hospitable living-room hearth, whose cheerful blaze, fed by fragrant, crackling juniper logs, formed a focal point of interest that tended to break down the barriers of reserve and to release the well-springs of thought and sentiment." He recalled sleeping out on the veranda. "Here I listened to the protean song of the mocking-bird, borne on gentle breezes laden with the voluptuous scent of orange blossoms, and repeatedly found myself so enthralled by the glamour of the moonlight that sleep was induced only at the cost of a distinct effort." It was a house designed to create such memories.

Retaining much the same atmosphere as when it was built, the study in Mary Darling's house still has the comfort of low beamed ceilings and the practicality of a well-lighted raised study alcove at the back of the room. A window seat in the bay window to the right, now hugging a desk, was removed by the previous owners.

CAMP HOUSE

In 1904, when the Camp House was built, one could stand on Grandview Avenue and look up through trees of oak, pepper, and box elder and see a rustic, board-and-batten structure backed by the quickly rising crags and ridge lines of the San Gabriel Mountains. Protected by the mountains but seemingly clinging to the land and spreading outward to the Pacific, the U-shaped house topped the uppermost part of a gently sloping spread of fifteen acres above the small village of Sierra Madre. Edgar Camp, a prominent lawyer from the Midwest, came to California with his wife, Theo, like so many others, for health reasons. With their two children, they looked for the dry, warm air of the upper hills and settled on Sierra Madre, a neighbor of Pasadena's. When *The Craftsman* magazine published an article in 1909 about this "mountain bungalow" designed by the architects "who are responsible for so much of the interesting domestic architecture of the Pacific coast," the accompanying photograph was of the massive chimney—its boulders piled one upon the next as though they had fallen into place from above, rising gently upward from a broad base, narrowing as it climbed to the sky. The house truly seemed to be built around the chimney, seemed in fact to grow out of it. In the simple board-and-batten, open-beamed living room, the fireplace also dominates, its fieldstones set into the hearth as though the mountain outside had become part of the home's inner world. Camp complained in his memoirs that "in one respect the house was not satisfactory; the heating by fireplace was insufficient for such a style of construction," and he "soon put in a furnace." But he also remembered how "in the evenings, we often gathered in the den and I read to the other three."

The main entrance opens onto a quiet patio, which is protected from street noise in the way the house wraps around it. Built a year after Greene and Greene first used this type of plan, the design encourages a free flow between the inside and outside worlds.

The Greenes designed some of the furniture, pieces that starkly contrasted with other commissions that same year. For Adelaide Tichenor and Jennie Reeve in Long Beach, Charles Greene had designed quite sophisticated variations on Gustav Stickley's Craftsman furniture, items that incorporated the expressed joinery, the slightly exaggerated mortise-and-tenon construction, and the projecting pegs of the Craftsman designs but were softer, their edges rounded and more oriental. The Camp House furniture, most likely designed slightly earlier, was simpler, more rustic and straightforward, and a better fit for the rural setting and simple lifestyle of the Camps. All the rooms except the kitchen were designed to open out onto the patio that was formed by the house's splayed U shape. This way of enclosing a courtyard or patio was something the Greenes had done for the first time only a year before, with the Bandini House in Pasadena (now demolished). Arturo Bandini, of an old Spanish California family, had asked the Greenes to build him a simple structure, a "California house," like one of the early adobes. In both the Bandini and Camp Houses, life was meant to flow freely between indoors and out: the patio formed just another living area for the family. Especially for the Camps, sitting in the patio with three sides of the house and the mountains behind them, facing the Pacific Ocean in the far distance, the family would have found a sheltering sense of peace.

71

Although the living room is now painted and the original field-stones in the hearth have been bricked over, the simple board-and-batten walls and the ceiling's open beams still give a rustic warmth to this "mountain bungalow" and complement the rugged stone fireplace, which is built of boulders from the nearby hills.

The Greenes returned in later years to carry out additional work for the Camp House. The stairway and built-in closets and drawers (above), added when Camp desired a second story, show the greater sophistication in joinery and finish the brothers were to achieve. Similarly, the finely molded plaster fireplace in the den (opposite), with its inset niches in place of a mantel, stands in arresting contrast to the earlier rusticity of the massive stone fireplace in the living room. Wood and stone, rough and smooth—they all fit together here.

REEVE HOUSE

T he house the Greenes designed in 1904 for Jennie A. Reeve, only their second commission outside the Pasadena area, was in the booming seaside resort of Long Beach. A relative of Mary Darling's, Reeve had the Greenes design a two-story shingle house for her on a corner lot. This commission came with the freedom to design both the house and its furniture, lighting fixtures, stained glass, built-in cabinetry, and landscaping. For the first time, the brothers had real control over a project, and they produced a small gem forecasting their masterpieces to come. ❧ Located three blocks from the beach, the house was made for the seaside. Unlike later Greene and Greene houses, where the entry leads back into a garden setting, here one enters an enclosed hall, warm and protective amid the lustrous Port Orford cedar. Straight ahead, past an art glass window that allows in light but not the street view, is the dining room. The table, chairs, and sideboard the Greenes designed for this board-and-batten room recall items published in Gustav Stickley's *Craftsman* magazine: simple mortise-and-tenon construction with cross pegging—the decoration all in the construction. The edges of the protruding pegs were carefully sanded to curve gently. Above the dining table hung a lantern, *Japonisme* in style, with a broad copper canopy over squares of Art Nouveau leaded glass patterned with flowers and vines. A similar lantern hung over the entry porch and another in the comfort of the living room inglenook. It was a house meant for the cold, foggy weather of a seaside town, yet on hot summer days the casement windows stretching across one of the living room walls could be opened wide to let in the ocean breeze. ❧ Reeve evidently relished the Greenes' accomplishment, because she went on to have them construct two investment houses, one in Long Beach, the other in Sierra Madre. In 1917 this house was lifted up off its foundation, placed on blocks, and offered for sale. Fortunately, it was purchased by an appreciative soul who had it moved nearby. A decade later, under Henry Greene's supervision, the same owner relocated it to its present site.

75

As appropriate for a house near the sea, the inglenook of Jennie Reeve's Long Beach home is a warm, comfortable, and intimate spot. Placed in a space partially under the staircase and protected by a built-in bookcase, it makes a perfect retreat on foggy days.

ROBINSON HOUSE

anging from the acquaintances of their father to the upper-middle-class burghers recently arrived in Pasadena, Charles and Henry Greene's client list finally reached aspired-for heights—wealthy tourists, often millionaires, wintering in the new town. One of the first of these clients in 1905 was the lawyer-financier Henry Robinson, who was a close friend of Herbert Hoover's and a member of the "banker's pool" that financed the 1920s boom in Los Angeles. The Greene firm was carrying out alterations to the home of Robinson's mentor, the millionaire David Tod Ford, when it was asked to build next door a "simple but spacious two-story, three bedroom home" for the Robinsons. Working on the Ford House was the contractor Peter Hall and an art glass artist, Emil Lange. So began a relationship that lasted through all the major Greene projects, one that provided the level of craftsmanship now associated with the work of Greene and Greene. Hall had moved as a child from Stockholm, Sweden, to Illinois, and became a master stair builder in Oregon and Washington; he and his brother John, a carpenter and cabinetmaker, came to Pasadena in 1892. Once they began their association with the Greenes, they stayed until the amount of work allowed them to establish their own shop. Emil Lange, from Milwaukee, worked closely with Charles Greene to refine interior features. Like Charles's own home, the Robinson residence looks out over the Arroyo Seco. As Henry Greene was to write in 1919, it "was placed on the western side of the lot in order to secure retirement and quiet and take full advantage of the views of the Arroyo." All the principal spaces—the living room, the dining room, and an enclosed porch—were carefully placed to frame the views. At two stories, the entry hall was the Greenes' most dramatic entrance to date. It is almost the same size as the adjoining dining room and about two-thirds that of the large living room. A stairway rises ahead, lighted by a hexagonal mahogany and stained-glass lantern well above. Shoulder-high wainscoting lines the staircase and the rest of the room, its lifting pattern—directing attention upwards—created by the cantilevered ascent of the stair risers. The motion is upward, up to the lightness of the second story and its east-facing windows.

Sited far from the street, Henry Robinson's house overlooking the arroyo was built of brick covered in stucco on the first floor, topped with a second story of English-style half-timber framing.

Off the entry are the downstairs rooms and the service wing, which is set at an angle toward the street. Straight ahead, to the left of the stairway landing, a door leads to a porch overlooking the arroyo. The dining room on the right and the living room on the left were suitable for entertaining, as Henry Robinson led an active retirement, involved in civic affairs and as a domestic and international representative for several presidents. On the east, with no view of the arroyo, is the coziest room, Robinson's den. Walled with bookcases and built-in cabinets and files, it has a fireplace of soft brown brick with a bench set at an angle to form an inglenook. The Robinsons' was a large house for a small number of people. The couple had no children and, except for their servants, lived in the house alone until their deaths. ❧ Later sold, the house was "modernized," the dining room gutted. The Greene and Greene–designed dining table, chairs, built-in china cabinets, and sideboard were removed, the chandelier relegated to the basement. Only a half century later was this room retrieved, through the efforts of the Gamble House of the University of Southern California and the Huntington Library, which had the dining room reconstructed in the Huntington's Virginia Steele Scott Gallery. The dining table is in the center of the room, its top shaped like a *tsuba*, the Japanese sword guards that Charles collected. At the base, a "cloud lift" motif and corbeled brackets reflect Charles's fascination with Chinese furniture and the joinery used in Japanese temples. Against the walls are the sideboard and the recreated china cabinets. The chandelier was the only adjustable-height fixture ever designed by the Greenes. Its iridescent glass reflects not just a new level of design for the Greenes but also a new pinnacle of craftsmanship achieved by those they chose to work with.

With its snug inglenook and beamed ceiling, the den is the only main room in the house that does not look out onto the arroyo. The fireplace of warm brown brick and the built-in bench of fumed oak, constructed with butterfly joints, are angled to the rest of the room, forming a little enclave of comfort in the spacious house.

Entering through the front door, one is immediately faced with a
dramatic stairway whose geometry is captured in a wood-framed
mirror (above). Ringed by a Japanesque railing, the landing (right)
wraps its way entirely around the open atrium. It was the grand-
est entrance hall and stairway the Greenes had designed to date.

BRANDT~ SERRURIER HOUSE

A modest Greene and Greene design, this inexpensive single-story cottage in Altadena, built in 1905, has interior walls that are simply boards held in place by battens, reinforced by strips of wood bolted together at plate-rail height. Despite its simplicity, care was taken in the placement of bolts and in the use of broad hinges on the doors. A. C. Brandt, the owner and a respected local contractor, had already worked with the Greenes on several houses. One of these was the home they designed the previous year for Lucretia Garfield, the widow of the assassinated president. Brandt did not move into his house, however, but sold it instead to a wealthy Dutchman, Iwan Serrurier, who had subdivided the property. Serrurier was already familiar with the Greenes' work, having hired them to design another house as a speculative venture. The house was later moved across the street, which is probably when the living room was extended and a garage added. Today passersby would never guess that it is a Greene and Greene, yet within one can find the care and attention of their best work.

One of Charles and Henry's simpler and less expensive homes, the cottage built by A. C. Brandt still shows outside (left) and inside (pages 84–85) the quality craftsmanship that Greene and Greene bestowed on their larger commissions. Straightforward clapboards on the exterior are echoed in the dining room's basic board walls.

BENTZ HOUSE

apan was introduced to the West Coast of America in the form of curios and art goods sold in 1876 from a shop in San Francisco's opulent Palace Hotel. In business two decades after Admiral Perry's 1854 arrival in Japan, this shop of an ambitious young Australian, George Marsh, was surely the first commercial outlet for such Japanese products in America. By 1900, up and down the California coast from San Francisco to Monterey, Santa Barbara, and Pasadena, small stores—located close to luxurious hotels catering to wealthy eastern tourists—were merchandising exotic objects brought back from Asia. Marsh had outlets in each of these resort towns, near shops operated by his competitors, including the brothers Nathan, John, and Philip Bentz. The Bentz brothers' store in Pasadena was across the street from the prestigious Hotel Green and little more than a block from the Greene and Greene office. Surely Charles must have haunted this shop, searching out the exotic, fingering objects, gazing at the woodblock prints, and leafing through the books on Japan that were loaned to interested customers. By 1900 John Bentz was ready to build his own building for the store, up a block and across the street, and it was to the Greenes he turned to implement what was really his design. If the building were still standing today, it would be nothing recognizable as the work of Charles and Henry. Like many of the newcomers to Pasadena, Bentz tried his hand at real estate investment. According to his daughter Helen, when the lots on his thirty-two acres were not selling well, Bentz in 1906 decided to have the Greenes build a model home "on the worst lot," saving the best lot to build their own home later on. Much to the disgruntlement of his wife, Louise, only the first part happened. The model house was built, "and we lived there forever," Helen recalled.

Towering over the Bentz House today, an old oak tree (opposite) was planted by John Bentz's daughter Helen when the house was built in 1906. Bentz intended the move to the house to be temporary, but he grew to love it so much that he spent the rest of his life here. In the living room (above), a bank of tall windows rises nearly from floor to ceiling to bring in warm sunshine and light. Opening off the near end of the room is an L-shaped porch that wraps around from the front of the house to the side. It was a model home in every respect.

87

efitting a model house, it was not overly wrought, but it was without question, the daughter remembered, a house that her father loved. Two stories high with only eight rooms under a single gable, this simple box was expanded outward with what were becoming Greene and Greene trademarks: a trellis that extended to one side and an open second-story porch off the upstairs hallway. The exterior was shingled, the interior painted in subdued colors balanced with woodwork left in its natural tones. 🌿 Louise Bentz was less enthusiastic about the house. "Mama was cross," the daughter noted, "because he had never let her build over on the point." So when John Bentz died in 1928, she promptly brought a painter to the house and "covered everything with off-white paint. Even the brick fireplace. Everything. Just everything...," the daughter said. 🍃 The interior remained covered with paint until the mid-1970s, when the new owners went to work to bring it back, stripping the wood and removing layers of paint to find the original colors. Today the wood of the dining room walls is rubbed back to its original luster, the fireplace is again a natural brick, and the walls are painted once more in the subdued colors the Greenes would have approved of.

Left unpainted when first built, the woodwork in the Bentz House was turned to white by Louise Bentz after her husband died. New owners have restored the wood to its original condition and repainted the walls in the natural colors the architects preferred.

DᵉFᵒRᴇST HᵒUSE

aroline DeForest lived only a short time in the house that the Greenes designed for her in 1906 before selling it to two sisters, Isabell Tabor and Agnes Tabor Vanderkloot, who lived here for a very long while. It was seventy-five years before their heirs put the house back on the market in 1986. These years took the house safely through that long period when the Greenes were forgotten and when homeowners painted woodwork white, installed track lighting, and ripped out built-in china cabinets. As though sealed in a time warp, this house was preserved. 🌿 Designed to be protected from the hustle and bustle of Pasadena, the small residence was set back on its lot. The ridge of the gabled roof runs across the short length of the house parallel to the street, allowing the long, gradual slope of the roof to drop down to the street side and providing cover from the urban madness. At the back of the house a few steps lead to a covered porch and the doorway, which opens directly into a living room that flows almost without transition across the width of the house to a dining area. Because of the way the land drops away steeply at the back of the house, this most social yet private area is given a majestic view south over the San Gabriel Valley. On the living room half of the house, a porch provides a place from which to enjoy this vista; on the dining room half, a bay window with a window seat looks out over the tree tops. Maintaining this sense of privacy, the rooms closest to the street are the kitchen and a downstairs bedroom, used for a maid or guests. 🌿 The sitting area next to the fireplace, the original brass wall sconces, the unchanged board-and-batten cabinets in the pantry and kitchen—all show how careful the Greenes' design work was even when they were not allowed the budgets of the Gambles or the Blackers. The soft warmth of the Port Orford cedar used for the paneling, beams, and detailing still resonates. Despite the massiveness of the fireplace, the burnt-red brick gives comfort to the small living room rather than dominating it. Even the kitchen, with its original wide porcelain sink and wood counter tops, shows the care the Greenes took to couple utility with a refined artistic sense.

The shower of lights over the dining room table (opposite), based on a chandelier Greene and Greene designed for the Duncan-Irwin House, replaced the original fixture—which was melted down as the sisters' contribution to World War I. It was probably just a simple device with commercial sockets and globes in any case. Like everything else in the DeForest House, the new chandelier seems to have always been here. The sisters' family kept the house for seventy-five years, never painting its Port Orford cedar woodwork (page 92), never altering or removing original built-in features such as the bench by the fireplace and the brass sconce above it (page 93). All was preserved in place.

94

Few Greene and Greene kitchens remain intact today, but the DeForest House's original porcelain sink and wood counter (above) survive for continued service. Outside, a sheltered pathway runs alongside the house (right), ensuring privacy and quiet as it leads one away from the busy Pasadena street to the main rooms at the back of the residence. There, residents and visitors alike are rewarded with a majestic view over the San Gabriel Valley.

BOLTON HOUSE

Already happy Greene and Greene clients, Dr. William and Alice Bolton in 1906 asked the Greenes to design another house, on the shoulder of a slight hill overlooking Pasadena's city center. Their earlier home was built in 1899, before the brothers had developed the sureness of style evident in the second residence. As construction of the two-story house began in July 1906, the Boltons ordered a number of pieces of furniture—for their living room, dining room, and entry hall—but then suddenly, before the house was finished, Dr. Bolton died. Only the dining room furniture had been completed.

Protected under a sheltering gable, the house's massive front door (above) is made of Port Orford cedar with panels of teak and art glass designed by Charles and executed by Emil Lange. Immediately off the entrance is a shingled veranda (right), which was enclosed by Henry in 1926 but then reopened as part of the 1979 restoration.

is widow moved east and rented the house to Belle Barlow Bush, who liked what had been done so far. She went ahead and had most of the remaining designs built and then commissioned Charles Greene to design other pieces such as a delightful bumble-bee clock, picture frames, and curio cabinets. The motif used in the clock and elsewhere—small bees of inlaid ebony—represented the initials of her name: BBB. She remained a faithful patron of Charles's, even having him design bookplates for her after she moved to Boston in 1914. ❧ The house was sold in 1917 to James Culbertson's sisters, Cordelia, Kate, and Margaret, who had decided to move from their 1911 Greene and Greene home, a house twice the size. They quickly commissioned the architects to make additions and alterations adding about a thousand square feet. ❧ New owners in the 1950s painted white all the Port Orford cedar and mahogany woodwork, and they removed the glass lanterns and the two fireplaces faced with Grueby tile. A local college later used the house as a warehouse and book depository. Soon scheduled for demolition, the house was saved only when the City of Pasadena and the Pasadena Historical Society took an eleventh-hour stand.

After being painted white in the 1950s, the Port Orford cedar woodwork in the entry and staircase (left) was restored to its natural finish two decades later when a saviour stepped in to rescue the Bolton House. In the living room (pages 100–101), French provincial wallpaper was pulled off the walls, exposing the colors chosen by the Greenes. The fireplace and other key features have been rebuilt to return the interiors to their original appearance.

In restoring the dining room (above and right), the decision was made to use a board-and-batten style of mahogany paneling, as the Greenes chose for the entry, rather than to recreate the large panels of Honduras mahogany veneer used originally on the walls.

A young man purchased the Bolton House in 1979 and spent the next nine years doing what, as he has put it, was "better described as a resurrection than a restoration." The roof was leaking. The plumbing was in such bad shape that dripping water had rotted out large holes between the floors. Hand trucks and fork lifts used when it was a book depository had left hundreds of dents and gouges in the walls and floors. In the living room, about all that remained were the windows. When he pulled down the French provincial wallpaper put up in the 1950s, however, the owner found not only the original colors on the sand-finished plaster walls but also the unpainted outlines of the original box beams, header trim, and other ornamentation, allowing him to recreate what the Greenes had intended. Behind the French provincial mantelpiece and the plaster was original Grueby tile on the chimney cheek. All the tiles had been removed from the hearth, but a local Arts and Crafts collector had enough matching Grueby tile to replace the discarded originals. The current owners take seriously their guardianship and are furnishing the house with Arts and Crafts pieces appropriate to the Greenes' work, so that it is finally being cared for as it deserved to be from the beginning.

Left a mere shell of a house after years of misuse as a book depository, the Bolton House's Greene and Greene features had to be either restored or recreated. Original bathroom fixtures upstairs (opposite) were saved. In the living room, a bench of Honduras mahogany was built in (top left). Port Orford cedar in the stairway was resuscitated (top right), as were the handsome built-in cabinets and drawers upstairs (above left). A dressing table in a design of which Charles and Henry might have approved (above right) was added next to a bathroom.

DUNCAN~IRWIN HOUSE

The Duncan-Irwin House in Pasadena begins deep in the canyon that runs next to it, starting with the age-rounded stones embedded in the almost dry creek bed and continuing upward, through native oak trees, up the steep side of the chapparal-covered canyon to where the land levels off and the first human artifacts are met: the roadway, originally a dirt path, and an outer retaining wall of ivy-covered arroyo stone. Civilization is engaged here, at a stretch of lawn with carefully placed Japanese stone lanterns. Massive eucalyptus trees rise from the mown grass. More of man's work shows in a foundation wall, a meandering composition of clinker brick embedded with boulders from the creek bed. Lifted above the lawn by the foundation wall are terraces to cross before entering the house, which is partially shaded by a pergola and the overhang of the second-story porches. Inside are rooms of restrained, soft coloration. The woods are all hand rubbed. Plaster panels present subdued earth colors to balance the darkness of the woodwork. This is a house that begins in nature and, by design, is gently transformed into a refined serenity.

The original house was not designed by the Greenes, however. The owner, Katherine Duncan, probably had it moved to the site overlooking the arroyo about 1901. Parts of the original house can still be found in the present-day structure: a coffered ceiling in a front room, a bay window in the living room. But the Greenes accomplished so much here—in the first additions and alterations for Duncan in 1903, and then, in 1906, in refinements for a new owner, Theodore Irwin—that it is difficult to isolate non-Greene elements. The house has a completeness of design, a unity and spirit, that makes it one of their masterworks.

107

With its open timbers, the covered terrace (opposite) provides a comfortable outdoor living space appropriate for the temperate California climate. Although Katherine Duncan's original house was not designed by Greene and Greene and has been added onto and altered over the years for different owners (above), the changes were so pervasive and subtle that the house became one of the Greenes' best works.

From the rugged world outdoors to the inner peace of the house: a careful transition progresses (left) from a retaining wall of arroyo stone, followed by a smooth lawn border, and then a terrace wall of clinker brick and stone. With a gnarled wisteria vine growing up around it, a pillar of arroyo stone and clinker brick alongside the entrance steps (above) holds up one end of a pergola that stretches out from the house. Every detail has its own role to play.

The original residence was a simple foursquare, but the house as it grew under the Greenes evolved into two stories built around an inner courtyard. All four sides of the courtyard have French doors, which open into an entry room, the music room, the downstairs guest bedroom, the dining room, and the breakfast room, making this an oft-used passageway in warm weather when the doors are left ajar. From any of the rooms can be heard the gurgling of the water in the goldfish pond. 🍃 No doubt because of the expanding nature of the design—more so than in any other house the Greenes were to design—the rooms in the Duncan-Irwin House avoid strict definition. There are three front doors, any one of which the uninitiated visitor might justifiably take as a primary entrance. One door opens directly into a denlike room with a clinker-brick fireplace and a window seat. Another leads into a true entry, from which the staircase rises to the second story. The third door, on the other side of the house, uncovers another true entry set between the living and dining rooms, a small room with French doors opening onto the courtyard.

Spaces meander—from room to room, around the courtyard, from music room to living room, through the entry to the dining room, past the breakfast room to the kitchen, then down a short hallway to a sitting room that looks through the wisteria-covered pergola. Beyond the guest bedroom is another entry, and then back to the music room. It is easy to stray out to the veranda, to return through another door, or to rest a while looking out to the mountains. ❦ Places abound to sit alone: in a Stickley rocker before the clinker-brick hearth of the intimate front room or in another of the rockers looking out a bay window. In the music room is a Morris chair with a table piled high with books and French doors leading to the courtyard. On a winter afternoon it is easy to snuggle up with a blanket in the cushioned window seat overlooking the arroyo. When several people gather, for this is above all a family house, they gravitate toward the main fireplace in the living room and the settle and two Morris chairs positioned around the blazing fire. ❧ In summer, breezes come easily through the open doors. At night, the sounds of wildlife are audible in the arroyo. A stillness, a quietude, reigns over this house, a sense of oneness with nature.

110

On warm summer days, life flows easily between inside and outside through French doors opening onto the courtyard (above). From the dining room (right), there is an openness to the house that allows one to move easily from room to room (pages 112–13).

Vertical slit windows in the staircase (top) echo the narrow slots in the banister while they light the way upstairs. Another narrow niche, in the living room fireplace (above), was surely intended by the Greenes to hold the tools for this massive masonry hearth (right). What was once an upstairs bedroom (pages 116–17) is warmed by a vivacious tile fireplace and now serves as a work-room for the current owner, who is a weaver and textile artist.

To reach the attic, a ladder designed by the architects just for that purpose (opposite) is kept ready for use, hanging on a nearby wall on the second floor. In this upstairs bedroom (above), as in each room of the Duncan-Irwin House, a refined simplicity reigns—achieved through simple fixtures and a spare but careful use of natural hand-rubbed woods, all balanced by subdued earth-tone colors for the walls. The aesthetic of the Japanese teahouse is evident throughout the house, a feeling that the Greenes were so clearly trying to achieve.

The prominent retaining wall of clinker brick and large arroyo stones (above), now a signature of the house, came about with the great expansion the Greenes undertook in 1906 for the second owner, James Neill. Josephine van Rossem's original small house grew larger and more assured as the Greenes strived to meet the new owner's needs. Shingles covered clapboards, a band of casement windows along the front replaced a bay window, and a Japanesque pergola over the driveway (opposite) demonstrated the brothers' growing maturity.

VAN ROSSEM~NEILL HºUSE

In 1903 the young, well-to-do widow Josephine van Rossem commissioned Greene and Greene to build, as an investment property, a two-story house not far from where she already lived on Arroyo Terrace in Pasadena. It was a simple seven-room box of a house, perfect for a rental property. Four bedrooms were upstairs; the living room downstairs occupied the front half facing the street, the dining room and kitchen the back half. The exterior was finished in plain horizontal clapboard siding, and the interior was done with natural redwood board-and-batten wainscoted walls, with a frieze of burlap.

This unaffected simplicity was carried through to the low ceilings of rough-sawn beams stained in soft brown that formed the floor for the bedrooms above. This modest rusticity was not solely the result of cost considerations—the house was only a few steps from the path to creekside picnics in the civilized wilderness of the arroyo. Even the street was a tree-lined dirt road that would not be paved for years. The side entrance sheltered the house from the road's dust. Not burdened with an entry, the living room at the front of the house had room for a bay window with a cozy seat and an open view of the mountains.

When James Neill bought the house from van Rossem, he had the Greenes make considerable alterations in 1906, changes that reflected the refinements of their maturing architectural style. The clapboards were covered with shingles, the roofline grew extended eaves, the main entry was moved to the front of the house (where the street was now paved), and a pergola over the driveway was built of timbers in an openly expressed style that reflected the Japanese temple architecture that Charles so loved. Replacement of the front bay window with a linear band of casement windows under an elbow-braced planter box produced a newly horizontal look. ❧ The most striking change was the distinctively Greene and Greene arroyo stone and clinker-brick wall fronting the property. Constructed the same year as the fireplace for the nearby Cole House, the base of the wall begins with large arroyo stones, boulders so carefully placed that they seem to have just come to rest there; then small stones and clinker brickwork thrust upward, obviously placed by hand but rising entirely naturally. "With its field stones," Charles wrote in 1908, the wall "is too heavy for the house but it affords the much needed privacy to the little garden overlooking the street." The neighborhood now built up, the city grown and modernized, this wall of heavy fieldstones and brick gives a greater sense of security and protection to the small house than was probably necessary in 1908. ❧ Reflecting changing tastes, the house again underwent a major renovation in 1925. The natural wood walls inside were covered with paint, the shingled exterior was stuccoed over. For fifty years the house remained in this condition until finally, in the mid-1970s, it was purchased by Randell Makinson, then the curator of the Gamble House, who restored it to its 1906 appearance.

A simple, rustic ambiance can be found in places such as the living room. Here, the ceiling is made of rough-sawn beams, while the wainscoted redwood walls are basic board and batten. Little changed during the Greenes' 1906 work, this part of the house remains a testament to the elegant simplicity of their initial design.

When the Greenes altered the Van Rossem–Neill House in 1906, they incorporated square Chinese tiles (above), which they used in many of their designs during this period. Installed here for both light and ventilation, they have counterparts outside in the massive clinker-brick and boulder retaining wall on the terrace. Another stylized pattern in art glass inset into the front door (opposite) casts a soft light on the Port Orford cedar woodwork of the interior. Painted over in the 1920s, the wood had to be stripped and refinished by later owners.

BLACKER H°USE

When the English Arts and Crafts architect C. R. Ashbee visited Pasadena in January 1909, he justly observed about Charles that "the spell of Japan is on him. . . . " Ashbee was not alone in noting the Japanesque nature of the Greenes' work, which had elicited similar observations since it was first widely published in 1906. By 1909 *House Beautiful* had published "A House in Japanese Style," a feature on the commission the Greenes regarded as their masterpiece, the Blacker House of 1907. This house of wood built for a wealthy lumber baron's family in Pasadena is the first of what the scholar Randell Makinson has called Greene and Greene's "ultimate bungalows." It actually had more to do with Boston and the Aesthetic movement's fashion for *Japonisme* than it did with either Japan or the simple life espoused by Gustav Stickley and the American Arts and Crafts movement. A lion's leap from the subdued Japanese aesthetic achieved just a year before at the Duncan-Irwin House, the Blacker House nonetheless shares a remarkable number of exterior similarities with the earlier one: the use of clinker brick and shingles, porte cocheres that jut out, second-story porches with Japanesque railings, gables and bands of casement windows, terraces, and especially exposed timbers. But at the Duncan-Irwin House, these exterior elements became part of the gentle transition from the landscape to the interior, from nature to the comfortable world of the house. Here these features are more formal and used with such force that they extend the house into the landscape rather than make it disappear into nature. The house occupied its position on its six and one-half acres of landscaped gardens in a stately, almost baronial manner.

Charles Greene made sure that the spell of the Orient suffused the Blacker House. Subtle Chinese "cloud lifts" rise in the door lintel, and hanging lanterns demonstrate that Japan was never far from his mind. When the house was completed, it was possible to sit here on the back terrace and contemplate Japanese-style gardens as well.

126

An inspired statement of the romantic exoticism of the East awaits at the entrance. On the porch the broad teak door jambs hold aloft a double lintel like a Japanese *torii* (temple entrance). Climbing vines in the opalescent glass, gray lines of lead, bowed mahogany stiles—all create an effect of lightness against the solid door. Inside, the hammered glass showers its golden radiance. The entry room is immense; many Pasadena houses would have fit inside. To the right is the dining room, to the left the living room, and ahead, through French doors, is the courtyard. Beyond was what *House Beautiful* called "the Japanese garden and grounds." ✿ The interior plan was not Greene and Greene's. The 1906 San Francisco earthquake rattled Robert Blacker's confidence in the design of his original architects,

Hunt and Grey of Pasadena, so he hired the Greenes instead because of their engineering skills, largely Henry's. Beyond retaining the interior layout and corner siting, he allowed the Greenes their freedom. ✿ A pointed bay of six French doors in the living room directs the view outward, to what were once the gardens and the lily pond (more a free-form lake), and then to the small Japanese gazebo beyond. At night the lake and the lilies in essence came into the room itself, where on the ceiling, between the beams, a bas-relief pattern of lilies and ripples was covered with gold leaf. Indirect light from lanterns made the room iridescent. Henry is said to have visited the house later and found the gold leaf covered with green paint. He stood there and wept, vowing never again to set foot in the house.

Set facing the San Gabriel Mountains, the house has a dramatic sixty-foot-wide porte cochere (above) that spans the circular driveway on the right and, on the left, a graceful second-floor balcony that shades the living room terrace. The entire exterior (opposite) is clad with thirty-inch green-stained split cedar shakes, with mahogany framing the casement windows. Wood is used sumptuously in the house, notably in the immense, teak-paneled entrance hall (pages 130–31). Crowning the ten-foot space is a ceiling made of Port Orford cedar.

After 1947, when both Robert and Nellie Blacker were gone, the postwar economy led the estate's executors to subdivide the property into seven lots. This left the house without a garage or keeper's cottage on just an acre and a quarter. The furnishings were sold off—placed on the front lawn for passersby. Following several other owners, the house was purchased by a Texas rancher and antiques collector who realized that the $1.2 million price was less than the value of the Greene and Greene–designed fixtures still inside the house. He stripped it of about seventy fixtures, including the front door, art glass windows, and five dozen of the original lights. This desecration prompted Pasadena to enact a city ordinance to prevent such destruction. ❧ New owners are renewing the Greenes' romantic world—their complete vision of design and craftsmanship—down to reproductions of the lighting fixtures that were removed and the furniture that was sold off. The Greenes always called this house their masterpiece. Now it is possible once more to understand why.

A fireplace in one of the Blacker House's upstairs bedrooms (opposite) captures the elegantly whimsical side of Charles's approach to architecture: trailing flower stems created by a mosaic of tilework wander down into the hearth, and wisps of smoke arise in the hood's metalwork. Recalling the stylized waves in a Japanese woodblock print, a baseboard patterned with rolling waves seems to flow upward, following the graceful rise of the grand staircase.

Passing through iridescent glass in both the window and the hanging Japanesque lantern, sunlight warms the teak paneling and woodwork of the second-floor landing (left). Gold-leafed water lilies in bas relief (top), which adorn the living room frieze and ceiling, evoke memories of the flowers once found in the Japanese pond outside the Blacker House. Still in the downstairs bathroom (above) are the original shower, pedestal sink, and bathtub.

RANNEY H°USE

Set slightly back from the street on the corner of Pasadena's busy Orange Grove Boulevard and the quieter Arroyo Terrace, Mary Ranney's house was the last of the cluster of Greene and Greene houses built in the Park Place Tract. The area, later dubbed Little Switzerland, was built up around the covered reservoir dug by the early settlers to create a water supply at the edge of the arroyo. The center of town was a few minutes by carriage, yet a hike down the canyon and up the arroyo led to a wilderness that Theodore Roosevelt said "would make one of the greatest parks in the world." ❧ Within three years of its construction in 1907, the two-story Ranney House was written about in an *American Homes and Gardens* article on "California Bungalows Costing One Thousand Dollars Upwards," a title that may have presaged the Greenes' later reputation for designing costly houses. The writer, Helen Lukens Gaut, called the house "rustic" and noted "a suggestion of old Swiss, also an intimation of Japan." The allusion to Switzerland came surely from the overhanging second story that was supported by stained redwood timbers, but the reference to Japan may have emanated from Charles Greene himself. In later years, after having moved to Carmel, Charles wrote: "People of Pasadena called my first group of successful houses little Switzerland—from my own understanding there was nothing Swiss about it—It all started from my interest in Japanese early temple design. I considered that they, in that simple timber work, they were the supreme masters. . . . " Without doubt the house was simple, built under broad eaves with "weathered redwood shingles," broken by "rough redwood timbers" on the outside. Inside, Gaut wrote of "the absolute simplicity of its finish and furnishings," observing that "the woodwork is all built on straight, craftsman-like lines."

137

Built in an area of Pasadena that came to be called Little Switzerland, Mary Ranney's house evokes images of Swiss architecture in its overhanging second story, which is braced by projecting redwood timbers. An "intimation of Japan" comes from its paneled teak and white pine door and its Japanese-style hanging lantern.

he client for this simple home was a college-educated woman who had recently moved to Pasadena from Chicago with her parents and started working for the Greenes. Already thirty-six, just a year younger than Henry, she must have had some past experience that the Greenes valued. It is possible that she worked on the design of her own home; later that same year her name was listed on another set of plans, for Charles W. Leffingwell's ranch bunkhouse in Whittier. This was unprecedented. Of all projects produced in the twenty-eight years of the Greenes' practice, these plans were the only ones to bear a name other than the Greenes'. Ranney did not stay long with the firm—within a few years she had gone on to establish a private college preparatory school for girls in Pasadena. The house was rented out, then went through a number of owners and gradually deteriorated. The landscaping had become so overgrown by 1983, when it came on the market again, that branches and foliage reached up to the second floor. A young architect living nearby who had fallen under the spell of Greene and Greene happened to see the "For Sale" sign. He promptly organized a partnership of professionals, two architects, a landscape architect, and a general contractor, who bought the house. The partners spent weekends and evenings over two and one-half years working to restore it. They stripped and refinished the major wood elements where they were salvageable, and where not parts were replaced using comparable woods. The Port Orford cedar of the entry hall, for example, was brought back to its original luster, but the front door was beyond repair and was exchanged for a new teak-paneled door. The redwood shingles on the exterior were restained, and a new cedar roof replaced the old. The reservoir is no longer behind the house—condominiums have arisen there instead. Automobiles, not horses, create the street noise. Even so the Ranney House today offers a quiet haven of simple dignity.

A swimming pool was added during the house's restoration in 1985. Its irregular shape and use of local arroyo stone help it achieve a pondlike feeling appropriate to a Greene and Greene house. Also part of the addition was the redwood deck overlooking the pool.

As part of the restoration, all of the Port Orford cedar woodwork in the house had to be stripped of paint and refinished. Rising up to a second-floor landing, the stairway (left) is well lighted by a double set of casement windows. The stair is shielded from the entrance hall by a built-in bench across from the front door (above).

GAMBLE HOUSE

In a relatively short time, over just seven years, the Greenes designed the great majority of homes in a small Pasadena neighborhood. Each house was individually—uniquely—designed for its owner. The last of these commissions, a winter home completed in 1908 for the Cincinnati Gambles of the Procter and Gamble Company, is the only Greene and Greene house now open as a museum. ❧ Experiencing the Greenes' work for the first time can be visually overwhelming. If a visitor touring the house tries to reach out and gently rub a hand along the entry hall table or pull open a drawer to examine the joinery, one of the eagle-eyed docents is likely to protest. Only when walking up the staircase are guests allowed, even encouraged, to feel and caress the well-polished mahogany of the banister, to see the sublime care that was taken with the finish. ❧ Visitors may wonder what it would be like to live in such a work of art—to sit, for example, in the dining room, your back to the built-in buffet, where Mary Gamble surely sat to be served dinner nightly with her husband, David, and two sons? To be able to gaze out the window, to see the greenery and the ridges beyond the canyon, straight ahead to the lantern-lit terrace, through the entry hall, toward the inglenook in the living room, softly bathed in a golden light by two lanterns hanging from the beams? After dinner, there might be time for reading aloud, the children nestled with pillows on the inglenook benches, or for a game of whist under three hanging mahogany and opalescent glass light fixtures.

With its projecting beams and broad overhangs to provide shade from the California sun, the Gamble House recalls the Japanese temples that so fascinated Charles. The architects planned the gentle rise to the front lawn to hide the driveway from the road, giving the impression that grass continues all the way to the steps.

At night these hanging lamps in the living room cast their strongest light, a gentle warmth that moves upward to reflect on the ceiling and then in all directions. Shadows remain in corners, under tables, and on the upper walls of the bay and inglenook, where the light cannot reach around the trussed beams. Only a hint of the trailing-vine design in the fireplace's iridescent glass mosaic remains. Charles Greene's frieze carved in the redwood that circles the room, in the style of a Japanese *ramma,* is lost in the darkness. The coziest room in the house is David Gamble's study, off the entry hall. Even though retired from Procter and Gamble, he needed a place to meet people and write letters. The Greenes designed furniture for this room, but instead Gamble wanted familiar pieces and brought out a rolltop desk and a Morris chair from his study in Cincinnati. The fireplace would be too large for this room were it not for the fact that the room is really part of the fireplace. The pressed-brick chimney breast rises upward, arching outward as it rises to meet the metal-strapped ceiling beams. The Gamble House remained in the family until 1966, when it was presented to the City of Pasadena and University of Southern California. Not only is it the only Greene and Greene commission open to visitors, it has also remained the best-preserved and most complete example of the brothers' architecture. Never was the woodwork painted over or the colors of the walls changed. The furniture today is placed as it was when the Gambles lived here. The carpets designed by Charles still cover the living room floor, and Mary Gamble's Rookwood vase still sits on her desk. Here everyone can experience the extraordinary attention to detail, the exquisite artistic vision, and the painstaking craftsmanship that characterized the work of Charles and Henry Greene.

There is no doubt here that one has arrived at an important home. For the teak-framed front entrance, Charles styled gnarled branches of an oak tree into sinuous patterns of iridescent glass that reach out to bathe the doors in a golden glow. With such mellifluous light, the hanging lantern seems almost superfluous.

144

The stepped banister of the stairway (opposite) creates a feeling of uplift, pulling one to climb three landings to the second floor. Tucked into the living room is the inglenook (above), a private space of benches and a fireplace bracketed by bookcases paneled in art glass. English Arts and Crafts devotees promoted inglenooks as a way to emphasize hearth and home. In the dining room (pages 148–49), the shimmering art glass introduced at the front door reappears in a screen of rose-patterned windows, a chandelier, and a pair of sconces.

Mary Gamble apparently never set foot in the kitchen of her house (above), but even here the Greenes' attention to artistic detail and function is more than evident. David Gamble, son of one of the founders of Procter and Gamble, liked to work in his study just off the entrance hall (opposite). The Greenes designed furniture for his private retreat, but he chose to have it furnished with pieces he brought with him from Cincinnati. Next to the built-in file cabinets, the pressed-brick chimney rises upward, arching outward as it meets the beams.

153

Julia Huggins, Mary Gamble's sister, lived in the house longer than anyone else. Her bedroom (opposite) opened out onto a healthful sleeping porch perfect for warm summer nights. Guest bedrooms (top left and right) were furnished with maple vanities and rockers as well as decorative tile fireplaces. In the master bedroom (bottom left) the bed and rocker have *tsuba* motifs, taken from the Japanese sword guards that Charles collected. An upstairs guest room sink (bottom right) was placed in a closet so that it could be closed off.

SPINKS HOUSE

Charles Greene was described at the beginning of 1909 as "a quiet, dreamy, nervous, tenacious little man." "Nervous" and "tenacious" were surely the most accurate adjectives. Producing designs for the firm's large houses as well as their interiors and fixtures and furnishings, he finally broke under the pressure. Needing calm and rest, he took his family to England for a seven-month sojourn. Henry had to step in to fill the chief design role that had been Charles's. 🐾 The younger Greene brother had a more refined and disciplined sense of composition. Compared to the almost capriciously lyrical, curvilinear lines and abstracted forms of nature that Charles loved to work with, Henry's style was much more linear. This distinction came out in houses completed during Charles's stay in England, not only the Spinks House in Pasadena but the nearby Crow-Crocker House as well, both built in 1909. 🐾 Constructed on pasture land just two years after and a short walk down the street from the Blacker House, the home for Margaret B. S. Clapham Spinks and the retired judge William Ward Spinks, who had just moved from Victoria, Canada, was more modest than its grandiose neighbor. Sited away from the street atop a slight rise that falls into a wooded canyon, the house is separated from the road by a broad lawn. Almost square in plan, its ten rooms rest securely under a single massive gabled roof with a low pitch. Henry's carefully considered design is obvious in the way he broke up the three-story rise of the facade—an inset entry stretches across two-thirds of the front, and the irregular placement of several bands of windows saves the rest from monotony. The back of the house is divided by carefully placed windows and doors plus a trellis on a porch, a good spot for surveying the gardens and wooded canyon.

154

Sheltered under a sweeping gabled roof with a low pitch, the house sits on a slight rise in the land, its rear facing a gentle slope that gradually drops off into a deep wooded canyon. A porch covered with a trellis opens off both the living and dining rooms and encourages appreciation of the gardens at the back of the house.

As with so many of the Greenes' houses, the original woodwork in the Spinks House was covered with paint over the years. But it has joined others in being restored (left), its Port Orford cedar painstakingly refinished by the current owners. Rising gracefully upward, the main staircase (above) is well lighted by a skylight.

Within the not-so-large house are many of the same design elements the Greenes employed on their larger, more costly constructions: windows and doors that pay attention to light and ventilation, careful transitions between inside and outside, an openness of space that invites comfort and repose, and a sensitivity to the use of materials. In the Spinks House and the one that Henry designed for Dr. S. S. Crow nearby, he placed a skylight to bring light into what would have been an otherwise dark hallway. Structural elements in these skylights use a geometric composition that, as with all of Henry's best work, is elegant yet simple and proves that he, as well as his brother, was capable of producing masterful designs.

PRATT HOUSE

Visitors come upon the Pratt House in Ojai almost as if by accident. It is not visible from the road. First into view are two large piled-stone pillars and then a drive that seems to wander through the contours of the landscape as a stream chooses the pattern of its flow. The house, built in 1909 in the Greenes' favored U shape, appears from the back side, showing its gentle bend. It seems to be two houses connected: a small, single-story, gabled bungalow on the right and a two-story structure on the left. The larger side is anchored at the farthest end by a sleeping porch and, closer to the parking area, by a massive clinker-brick and cobblestone chimney rising from the terrace that runs between the two wings. On the terrace is what looks like a hallway but is really a covered walkway joining the two parts. This is the entrance. 🏵 As with all the Greenes' "ultimate bungalows," coming through the front door of the Pratt House becomes an experience of entering a space where the natural world is integrated into the interior. In the others, each more urban than this, doors of art glass mark the entry, bringing the warmth of lighted color into a dark interior. Here the front doors are of simple uncolored glass; the muntins in the door frame form an elegant Japanese *torii* (temple entrance). Darkness is alleviated by French doors immediately opposite that open onto a rear terrace. Beyond is the uncultivated wildness of chaparral-covered foothills outside this small town inland from Ventura.

Set amid sun-drenched, rocky hills on fifty-two acres not far from the California coast, the house emerges naturally from the landscape. Only a single room wide, its splayed U shape follows the contours of the rise on which it sits. The overlapping gables of the various roof levels step up like the mountains rising behind.

158

he plan radiates outward from the entry at the bend of the house. On the left are the bedrooms, and on the right are the dining room, kitchen, and maid's rooms. One moves right away into what the Greenes called the living room but what is more a living hall as in large, Victorian shingle houses on the eastern seaboard. It is an entry room with a fireplace and seating and opens into the other rooms. Separated by only a doorway is the high-ceilinged dining room, and on the other side lies a hallway that gives onto a more intimate sitting room, the den, and a downstairs bedroom as well as the stairway to the second level. ❧ Carefully sited on fifty-two acres, on a ridge overlooking the Ojai Valley, this was without question a country home. It holds the vestiges of rusticity that the Greenes accomplished in their Bandini (1903) and Camp (1904) Houses but with greater refinement befitting the client. Charles Pratt was a wealthy New Yorker who was one of the founders of Standard Oil and a half owner of the nearby Foothills Hotel. He called his house Casa Barranca and used it for wintering in California. No doubt he was influenced in his choice of architects by his wife, Mary, who was the Vassar classmate of Caroline Thorsen and her sister, Nellie Blacker. ❧ On hot summer days doors and windows on the first and second stories—the house is only one room deep—can call up cross ventilation from fresh breezes. The broad overhang of the eaves helps cast shadows that likewise cool the interiors. Stepped up slightly by the clinker and cobblestone terraces, the house clings to the ridge, holding onto it as though it had always been there.

Broad roof overhangs, their rafters extended beyond the eaves (opposite), cast beautiful shadows on the walls of Casa Barranca, as Charles Pratt baptized his home. Fieldstones in the terrace wall (above) seem to have been put in place by nature, the bricks merely adding the designer's mark to what was already there. The house has no actual entrance hall: reflecting the casualness of the countryside, one enters the house without preamble directly into the living room (pages 162–63), which has a comfortable built-in bench next to the fireplace.

Trapezoidal in shape to accommodate the form of the house, the living room (opposite) necessitated a masterful composition of angles in its beamed and paneled ceiling. Equally adept was the Greenes' design for the octagonal light (possibly inspired by a Chinese paper lantern) that hangs from leather straps in the tall dining room (top left), their iridescent glass windows (top right), their fireplace brick in a chevron pattern (bottom left), and their leaded glass light fixture affixed to metal-strapped beams in the living room (bottom right).

Appropriately less ornate for the countryside, the pantry (left) and the curio cabinets in the living room (above) nonetheless bear the same refined craftsmanship and sense of design as the best of the Greenes' work. The master bedroom (pages 168–69) has the feel of a shipboard cabin, although much more spacious, because of its beamed ceiling and meticulously finished walls of Port Orford cedar.

THORSEN HOUSE

Diners at the Thorsen House in Berkeley feel perched above the street, looking through a bay window shaped like the stern of a ship. When the house was constructed in 1909 and before the neighborhood was built up, below was a panoramic sweep of San Francisco Bay and the small passageway to the sea called the Golden Gate. The ocean and all it represented was important to William Thorsen. His father, a sea captain, had left Norway at age fourteen to sail as a cabin boy. The son loved ships too and owned some himself. References to ships and the sea abound in the house. A nearly floor-to-ceiling oil painting of a harbor with sailing ships is framed in a Greene and Greene—designed box frame. Across the way are prowlike windows shaped in a V; the ridge beam running through them seems to form a bowsprit.

Proudly looking out toward the Golden Gate and San Francisco, this house is the most urban of Greene and Greene's "ultimate bungalows." The carefully crafted fence and gate into the back garden (above) is a delightful composition of positive and negative spaces. Steps (right) lead up from the street into a world set apart.

horsen was a lumber baron, as his father became, and his wife, Caroline, was the daughter of one of the great lumbermen of Michigan. The northern forests depleted, he moved west and became a partner in a northern California lumber business. For his second house in California, he turned to the Pasadena architects who had designed a home for his wife's sister, Nellie Blacker, and her lumber-baron husband, Robert Blacker. ❧ The Thorsen House is the only grand house of the Greenes set on a normal-size city lot. Configured in an L shape, the shorter leg rests on a main boulevard; the longer faces a side street, leaving a garden area protectively screened by the two wings. A wall of clinker brick, a small lawn area, and a sweeping set of brick steps give a small but definitive transition upward from the busy thoroughfare. The living room, entry, and dining room face the main street; the kitchen and servants' rooms are turned toward the side street. On the second floor, the master bedroom suite and the guest bedroom look onto the boulevard. Prow-shaped windows framing San Francisco Bay reappear in the master sitting room. ❧ The Thorsens lived in the house until their deaths, both of them in the spring of 1942. The furniture was removed the next year, and the house was put on the market. Set a stone's throw from the University of California on a street becoming known as fraternity row, it was quickly purchased by the Sigma Phi fraternity. Still there today, the fraternity has in recent years spearheaded a restoration and preservation campaign. In the summer of 1996 Sigma Phi and the Gamble House sponsored an exhibition that for the first time in more than a half century reunited the Greene and Greene–designed furniture with the house. The students painted the walls their original colors, and the pieces were placed as they were originally. More than eleven thousand people were able to visit this example of the Greenes' design genius.

Exquisite examples of design and craftsmanship achieved by the Greenes in the Thorsen House range from iridescent patterned glass in the front door and overhead lantern (opposite), to an inlay of ebony and fruitwood in the newel post of the staircase (right), to sconces and a built-in desk in the living room (pages 174–75).

Opening off the bedrooms of both William and Caroline Thorsen, a small sitting area (above) was formed in the hallway by placing a bay that can be closed off for privacy. It enjoys a lovely view of the gardens at the back of the house. The living room fireplace and its hearth (opposite) were faced with Grueby tile and fitted with a header inlaid with a bronze motif. Along the room's frieze border, Charles painted a composition of trailing roses designed to appear as if they were growing from behind braces holding aloft the scarf-jointed railings.

ANTHONY HOUSE

The plans for the Anthony House were dated December 24, 1909, the same day the Pasadena newspapers reported that "Charles Sumner Greene of Greene & Greene, architects, … has just returned from an extended tour of England and Europe." One can see the trip's influence in later houses by the Greenes, but this one was Henry's work alone—done entirely during Charles's absence—and demonstrated a masterful handling of elements the Greenes had already perfected. Henry's careful attention to detail can be seen inside. All the principal rooms are staggered so that windows on three sides allow in natural light. The living room and a small den face the street to form the short side of an L shape. Down the long side are the dining room, a pantry, the kitchen, and a maid's room. Doors in the living and dining rooms open onto a garden area private from the street. Despite having a maid's room and front and back staircases, it is still not an ostentatious house: the entry small, the fireplace, walls, and windows without the intricacy and costly craftsmanship of the Gamble or Blacker Houses. Yet craftsmanship is still a vital element. Doors are opened by sliding, spring-loaded latches. The Greene and Greene signature "cloud lift" motif appears in a reverse pattern in all the windows. Built originally on rapidly developing Wilshire Boulevard, by 1923 the house was in danger of being torn down. The silent film star Norman Kerry stepped in to purchase it and had Henry supervise a move to a quieter location in Beverly Hills. In conjunction with the move, Henry was able to design new landscaping. Earle Anthony, the original owner, was a Packard dealer who later had dealerships in northern and southern California as well as several radio stations. Although he turned to Henry Greene the next year for a home for his mother-in-law, he chose Bernard Maybeck to design a new home of his own on a fifteen-acre estate in Los Angeles. That elaborate manor was very different from what Henry Greene had provided him fifteen years earlier.

Simpler than the grand bungalows the Greenes had just completed in Pasadena, this house is entered up a short flight of stairs, under an open gable, and through a front door with only a small amount of art glass. But the rafters projecting beyond the eaves, rounded by hand, leave no doubt that it is the work of Greene and Greene.

As with all of the Greenes' work, no artifice is expressed in the interior design of the Anthony House. Ceiling moldings in the dining room (opposite) are simple runs of wood, and door and window lintels are extended around the room, creating rails from which to hang pictures. The walls are basic board and batten. In an upstairs hallway (above), rafters form the beams. Doors throughout are paneled redwood and are opened with sliding, spring-loaded latch handles. Even after a number of earthquakes, every door still hangs perfectly square.

The land on which the house was constructed drops away so steeply into a canyon in back that the rear wing (opposite) becomes two stories high, although at street level (above) the house appears to have been built all on one floor. Three sides of the U-shaped house surround a courtyard. A white wisteria-covered pergola (pages 184–85) across the open end provides even greater privacy and peace. Both its formal demeanor and its materials—the pale masonry topped by green tiles—set the house apart from other Greene houses.

CULBERTSON SISTERS HOUSE

After the Greenes finished the house and furnishings for James Culbertson's three sisters in 1911, along with extensive Italianate gardens, the cost of maintaining the property ended up being more than Cordelia, Kate, and Margaret Culbertson could afford. They sold it in 1917 and bought the much smaller Bolton House, also designed by the Greenes. The new owner, Mrs. Dudley Allen, was so impressed with the furnishings that within a week she went north to where Charles Greene was living in Carmel to talk with him about further work for the house. ❧ The last of the large commissions that Charles and Henry worked on together, the house is not one that many would recognize immediately as from the hands of Greene and Greene. Unlike the Blacker House across the street, the exterior is not redwood timbering and shingle with clinker brick and cobblestone; it was constructed of earth-toned Gunite,

a stuccolike concrete material applied with a pressure gun. The roof is of Ludowici-Celadon porcelain tiles glazed in variations of green with the occasional dash of burnt red. No art glass graces the house. Wood was used inside, but it was all painted. The furniture was more akin to Hepplewhite than Stickley and was upholstered in brocaded fabrics. Yet, as in all of their better work, that serene Greene sense of harmony permeates the house. ❧ Like many of the firm's earlier designs, the house is built in a U shape around a courtyard. From the entry on the side facing the street, windows present a composed scene: a courtyard with a tiled octagonal fountain. A wide hallway features windows and doors opening onto the courtyard on one side, the opposite wall finished in a soft, brownish velour. Where the hall meets the corner closest to the street, it widens into a gallery called the Garden Room that can be opened up to the outside by a sliding wall of glass.

Seen from the street the house's aura is of a Chinese temple, but by the time one explores down to where the extensive gardens used to be, the spirit—despite the oriental touches—is obviously more Italian than Asian. The land gradually drops down from the street into Oak Knoll Canyon, falling away at such a slope that, although the front wing of the house is at street level, there is room under the back wing for a ballroom complete with a stage. It was originally an open loggia overlooking the formal gardens, and beyond were steps and landings leading to a lily pond and grass court; the stairway, splitting at an upper landing to encircle the pond, left space for a classically designed, four-level fountain gurgling toward the lilies. ❦ One of the projects that Allen (later she married Francis F. Prentiss) commissioned Charles to do for her was to make two marble urns that still stand today on either side of the entry walkway. She warned Charles, after he submitted his bill, that in the future it would be advisable to be "somewhat definite in the cost of any undertaking" before, not after, charging her. The urns were not cheap, even in 1928, the year before the Great Depression hit—they cost her $1,916.75. ❦ Charles's response explains his attitude toward architecture. "Speaking of estimates," he wrote, "it seems to me that you do not know, or you have forgotten that your house and all in it were completed without an estimate and exceeded all expectations." This quality, he pointed out, is why her "fine discriminating sense singled it out from many others." He added that if she had come to him "to build the house, but had limited me to an estimate, 1188 Hillcrest could never have existed. . . . Business, I admit must be run upon business lines, but this is not business, this is the art of helping to make living pleasurable and beautiful beyond the merely useful."

187

An antique alabaster lamp, purchased by Charles on a special buying trip to New York in 1912 for the Culbertson sisters, hangs from the high vaulted ceiling of the entrance hall. The great height of the ceiling allowed room for impressionistic panels painted by Charles, copies of which now hang on the walls in the space.

A wrought-iron grille hung beneath an Istrian stone carving (above) leads to the former ballroom downstairs (right). The space was once an open-air loggia looking out onto the Italianate gardens and lily pond, which no longer exist. The only exposed timberwork is found on a porch (page 190) whose structural supports hold up the heavy tile roof. Corbels in the shape of musicians (page 191), designed by Ernest Batchelder, decorate the ballroom.

FLEISHHACKER HOUSE

When Mortimer and Bella Fleishhacker were looking for an architect to design their country home in Woodside, south of San Francisco, they thought the Greenes' work too Japanese. What they wanted was something English, cottagelike and thatched. But they were charmed by Charles Greene, who had recently returned from an extended stay in England. After Charles brought Henry Greene to meet the family, Mortimer Fleishhacker, a paper company executive, requested that in the future he deal only with the more engaging Charles. The children nicknamed the brothers "Green Greene" and "Pink Greene." Charles, of course, was the real Greene, and Henry was the pink Greene. So it was Charles who became the family architect in 1911, designing for them not only this large country house, anointed Green Gables, but also doing alterations for it later, adding the gardens and outbuildings, and remodeling their San Francisco home. ❧ The main house is placed on a hill roughly in the center of the seventy-five-acre wooded property. Although several houses have been built here for family members, no sign of these other habitats can be seen once the house is reached. The driveway ends at what seems to be the back of the house, the garage to the left, then the kitchen and service wing. For a country manor, the front entry is rather subdued. Through the entry hall and the facing French doors, out onto the back terrace, it becomes clear how magnificently the house is sited.

For more than twenty-five years, Charles Greene served as the family architect for Mortimer and Bella Fleishhacker, executing a series of commissions beginning in 1911 with the main house and immediate grounds (opposite), continuing with designs for a swimming pool in 1916, a card room complete with furniture in 1923, and a magnificent water garden (above) in 1927, whose double stone stairway leads sixty-five feet down to a Roman pond below. In 1928 Charles also designed a whimsical stone dairy house in which tea was to be served.

efore it was designed, according to the family, Charles would "sit on the little hill for hours and contemplate the scene and situation." Slightly down the hill where Charles must have been seated was a massive old oak tree, and it was here, around this tree, that Charles placed the house. The tree no longer exists, but when it did, family and visitors stepping onto the terrace would have passed to its right. The dining room doors at the other end of the terrace opened to the left of the tree. 🍂 From the terrace, the far view is of gray-blue mountains. Closer at hand, in the middle distance, are hills covered with woods and grass. Arrayed directly in front is the formal terraced lawn and gardens—two symmetrical brick pathways leading to a reflecting lily pond. Down a steep slope from the lawn and the pond, designed by Charles in 1927, a decade and a half after the house was built, is a stunning water garden. Its 300-foot-long pool ends in a series of arched columns built of stone, reminiscent of the Roman aqueducts and looking as though they had been there since ancient times. Moss is now embedded in the crevices between the stones, an effect that Charles must have wanted to achieve to make the tableau part of the landscape, as if it had aged with nature yet was better than nature alone could have achieved. A companion stone dairy house, in which Bella Fleishhacker had wanted to serve tea, was dubbed "Greene's Folly" because it was too distant to use. 🍃 A special relationship developed between the Fleishhackers and Charles Greene, that of patron and artist. It was a relationship that Charles spent his lifetime looking for and only rarely found. In this instance, once found it provided over a span of two and one-half decades an outlet for the creative work in which Charles excelled and produced a masterwork of architectural and landscape design.

At the end of the Fleishhackers' Roman pond, the arcade (right) has settled into a graceful patina of age. Charles enclosed an open sunroom to make a card room (pages 196–97), giving him the opportunity to carve a tooled-leather card table with chairs. He also carved the cabinet doors and frieze panels depicting exotic scenes on different continents. Because this was the only room with furniture designed by Charles, the family named it the Greene Room.

In this house the rooms have painted wood and soft-tinted plaster. Although the guest room interiors were designed by Elsie de Wolfe, Charles's genius is evident in the details. At the main stairway (above), windows are placed so that one climbs up into light. One of the downstairs guest bedrooms that must share a bathroom (right) has its own sink and mirror conveniently ensconced in a closet.

WARE HOUSE

reene and Greene designed just two houses in 1913. Although the firm would exist for the coming decade, in reality the brothers had already grown apart. Charles was taking determined steps to become a writer, and Henry was left to run the office. What work emerged was primarily Henry's. One of the year's two clients, Henry Ware, had come from Winnetka, Illinois, to Pasadena for health reasons. Ware asked for something similar to his English-style home in the Midwest. Charles probably would not have curbed his own artistic sensibilities so easily, but Henry met the owners' needs and requests with great competence, even though they certainly constrained the design. Where the Greenes' Phillips House of 1906 directly faced the street, the home they designed for the Ware family across from it on the same street was more private—one had to walk up the side of the property to reach the entrance—and more like some of their earlier work. Recalling James Culbertson's home from 1902, this house was plastered on the first story and shingled above, the second story slightly overhanging the first.

To ensure some distance from the street and its noise, the entrance of the house was placed along the side and down a brick path. The look is English—to please the owner, Henry Ware—and was achieved by pairing stucco on the ground floor with two projecting shingled stories above. Bay windows enliven the facade.

Always conscious of the need for light, Henry designed French doors that would open from the entry into the living room (above). The doors opposite lead out to a wisteria-covered pergola. So that Mary Ware would not be bothered by glaring lights, indirect lighting was placed in troughs behind the wood railings near the ceiling. In the dining room (opposite), which is more traditional than usual for the Greenes, the brothers' concern for fine craftsmanship shows in the fumed oak wainscoting and the fireplace of cast stone and Batchelder tiles.

hree steps up from the entry inside is what is called on the plans the "main hall," an open space with built-in bookcases and a staircase that rises grandly upward. It is impressive and formal, lacking the Greenes' usual openness to the outside and the sense of *Japonisme*. One can detect the brothers' Boston years here and the English sensibilities Charles brought back from his overseas travels. To the right of the entry is the living room, to the left the oak-paneled dining room. It is not a house immediately identifiable with the name Greene and Greene, until one begins to notice the details. In the dining room the fireplace glistens with Batchelder tiles and leaded glass shines in the windows. Grueby tiles enliven the living room fireplace, framed by a wire-brushed redwood mantel. Mary Ware had poor eyesight, so Henry designed for her a system of lighting troughs encircling the living room to provide a gentle, indirect light. Two generations of the Ware family fit comfortably into the house, which sufficiently met their needs that they lived there for seven decades, through three generations. The house is now under only its second set of owners and has gone through few changes. Original soapstone counters and a butler's pantry survive in the kitchen. The original gravity heater still gives out heat. An orange tree outside the living room predates the house, and the rose garden the Wares planted flourishes even today.

LADD H°USE

In 1913 Charles Greene was spending his time working on the immense Fleishhacker House in northern California. Henry Greene thus took the lead role in designing this house for the William Ladd family in Ojai, as he did with the Ware House in Pasadena. This commission reflects an intense attention to siting and a return to styles the brothers had developed and refined in the past. While the Ware House recalls what they had known in their Boston years, the Ladd house reverts, appropriately, to the rustic. ✿ This is not a house designed for formal entertaining but instead for countryside living. It is set next to the main road, but the driveway curves around the end of the house so that the entry is protected, located away from the street. Set high on a retaining wall of native stone is a meandering terrace, which wraps around the living room at the north end of the house. A number of terrace doors open into the living room, although the main entrance is through a simple door that leads into a long hallway running the length of the house's east side. It is not an entry for formal entertaining. Wide and well lighted, this hallway is still a hallway. Along it, on either side of the main staircase, are bedrooms. To the left down the hall is the living room, to the right the dining room and kitchen. The stair's steps ascend to the master bedroom, which takes up the entire second floor.

205

To extend life in the house into the picturesque Ojai Valley, a terrace outside the living area was built with stone hauled from the nearby hills. Tucked into the base of the terrace wall is a small chair also made of stone. The wall terminates in a vertical exclamation point: a rugged stone chimney that rises up through the roof.

Fitting for its countryside setting, the door to the house opens directly onto a hallway (above). Bedrooms and the stairway are across from the door, and the living room (right) is at the end of the hallway. Walls are simple board and batten, as appropriate for this version of the simple life. Craftsman-style furniture fits right in.

Up the road is the home the Greenes designed just four years earlier for the wealthy New York oilman Charles Pratt. Echoes of the Pratt House can be found in this design. Here is the same abbreviated second story for the master bedroom, the same gentle roof slope so reflective of the surrounding rolling hillsides of the Ojai Valley. Both houses have broad terraces overlooking the dry California landscape, and both, sited on slight rises, seem to cling to the terrain. Inside is the same use of board-and-batten walls, the same sensitivity in the placement of windows. ❧ No furniture or fixtures were designed for this house as they were for the Pratts'; obviously, the budget was not there, and possibly neither was the desire for such costly touches. What was designed, however, while simple, was appropriate and reflected the key elements of the best of the Greenes' work: the use of local materials, a sense of design that was both artistic and restrained, careful placement of the house on the land, and an inspired sense of interior space and light, all producing a home that is sheltering and comfortable yet open to the world outside.

JAMES HOUSE

I n 1916 Charles Greene decided to leave southern California behind and go to Carmel "to ponder life and art" in the pines. "Is there more in life than art?" he asked. "Is there anything in architecture without art?" He told his friends that he was giving up his work. "I broke my vow just once," he said, "for one house to grow out of [a] rock cliff overhanging the Pacific Ocean...." Greene lived the rest of his life in Carmel, where he did more work than this one house "overhanging the Pacific Ocean," but the James House was to be his masterpiece—the commission that in the end mattered most to him. Unfettered, he had the freedom he dearly desired. "I am everything," he wrote, "without office boys, draftsmen, and secretary." And without an on-site client. His patron, D. L. James, was an aspiring playwright, a wealthy merchant of fine imported china, glass, and silver who lived in Kansas City and came to Carmel only in the summer. Both he and his architect had visions of a bohemian refuge away from the rest of the world. Two days after the pair visited James's rocky point of land in Carmel in 1918, Greene showed James an impressionistic watercolor sketch of the house he envisioned. On the spot, James authorized Charles to proceed. But construction did not proceed as James imagined. When he returned the next June, he was shocked to find that work had been done only on the retaining walls and foundation. But what incredible workmanship! Charles "was passionate about getting the rock he wanted," recalled James's son Dan. And passionate about its placement. The granite was quarried a mile down the coast and hauled by horse-drawn wagon to the building site, where Charles would stand watch—and occasionally order demolition of whole sections of wall that had been built without his supervision. It was, Dan thought, as if Charles wanted the job to continue forever.

While regaining his spirit in England during a 1909 trip, Charles stopped to paint a watercolor of ruins at Tintagel castle on the Cornish coast. He recreated that romantic view in a portal at the James House (left), leading nowhere. Charles devoted four years to supervising construction of the house, rock by rock (opposite).

ames eventually insisted that the house be finished enough that the family could occupy it. Charles's furniture designs were never executed, and the upstairs study that James was to use for his writing was left off, but in the summer of 1922 the family was finally able to move in. The Jameses did not hold a grudge—they came back to Charles in 1937 to add the study, which was not completed until Elizabeth Gordon, the editor of *House Beautiful,* paid for the work to be done in 1956 so it could be featured in her magazine. ❧ The house today is protected from the busy coastal highway by a solid, high stone wall. Step through the wooden gate in the wall and the land drops gradually downward. Descend the stone path toward the house and the highway noise recedes, replaced by the rhythmic rolling rumble of the ocean. Seen from a boat, the house rises from the rocky cliff so naturally that it is impossible in places to tell where the bedrock ends and the foundation begins. Charles's masterpiece seems part of the landscape, of the pine trees, stone, and ocean. At the end of the stone path around the left of the house, there is only a waist-high rock wall as protection from the precipitous drop to the ocean. To the right are the house's massive walls, rough to the touch, the granite pieces layered in courses of an always-varying pattern, the broken edge of the stone exposed to the elements. ❧ A gate leads to another archway framing a vista through pines downward to the crashing ocean. The scene, like the archway, is carefully constructed. Its inspiration can be found in a spot high above the ocean along the rugged English coast of Cornwall. Relaxing there in 1909, Charles captured in watercolors the craggy shore as seen through an ancient stone archway of the ruins at Tintagel castle. This romantic vision is virtually recreated in Carmel. To do so was surely its only purpose—the archway leads nowhere; the path ends abruptly, and only the cliff and the ocean lie beyond.

Perched on its stony promontory in Carmel, the James House affords stunning views of the Pacific Ocean while it protects its occupants from the sea's sometime wrath. The front door opens onto a cloister-like courtyard, whose gentle bend reaches out to welcome visitors and offer the comforting security of a secluded space.

211

he courtyard is a haven from the elements and the entrée to the house, through simple, wood-framed, clear-glass doors. The interior is as formal as the exterior is picturesque and romantic. The thick and solid walls are plaster, soft-looking after the jagged stones outside. Marble is used for the sills and thresholds; teak frames the windows. Within the house, the landscape—nearly overwhelming outdoors—is reduced to manageable proportions. Through the entry, through three arches, through the library appears a large three-section window that offers a majestic view of waves crashing on rocks. A double doorway steps down into the living room. Across the room is another large window, another grand vista safely framed. The living room is not vast, but the act of descending its five steps, sheltered by the high redwood ceiling and refreshed with the vista of points distant, imparts a feeling of regal immensity. Nearby is the narrow intimacy of the library. Window seats on either end of the room bracket the fireplace, forming spaces where it is natural to pull a blanket around one's shoulders, read a book, or simply watch the endless cycle of crashing water. In acknowledgment of the often cold and foggy climate, there are many fireplaces. It is not a large house—only two bedrooms, a living room, a den, and the kitchen. When the Jameses invited dinner guests, they had to set up a table in the living room. But the house that Charles created for them invites clarity of mind and restfulness. With the fires lit, the wood crackles and the room smells of burning madrone logs. The waves down below make their own white noise. In this place, envisioned by an architect who was more truthfully an artist, one finds the peace and the refuge, the security and the beauty, for which Charles Greene spent his life searching.

Carefully placed stepping stones lead down the side of the house (opposite). Because of the way in which the wall rises from the ground, it is difficult to distinguish where nature's work ends and the architect's begins. The stone was laid in such a fashion (right) that it appears as if it simply flows up to and around the windows.

214

Soft plaster finishes inside (top) contrast nicely with the rough stonework outside. A tall arch frames the view from the living room into the library (above), punctuated by a band of limestone between walls and ceiling. The house had no dining room, so the Jameses made the living room (right) fill that function for dinner parties.

An openness is immediately apparent on entering the house. Across from the entry is the library, framed in three arches (left). To the right and down is the living room. In the main bathroom (above), a perfectly round shape, the bathtub and sink are made from carved stone. In the dressing room between the bedrooms (page 218), deeply cut arches mirror each other. The same arch reappears in the library window (page 219)—an incomparable yet supremely secure spot from which to monitor the comings and goings of the sea.

Charles's studio (above) was built as more than just a work place. It was meant to be a gathering spot for the community—a venue for concerts and lectures. For the walls, he cleaned old bricks salvaged from a hotel. Teak wood for the front door (opposite), hand carved by Charles, was given to him by a lumber company that was grateful for his past business. And now his unfinished roof has finally been tiled.

CHARLES GREENE STUDIO

hen Charles Greene moved his wife, five children, and a fox terrier to Carmel in the fall of 1916, the family lived in rented houses for the first four years until finally, in 1920, he built a simple redwood home. It was only in 1923, just a year after Greene and Greene was dissolved, that at the age of fifty-four he was able to build something for himself—a studio in which he could work, think, meditate, and at times gather around him those who were of like mind. 🍃 The ideal of a studio conveys the image of an artist: painters' smocks, skylights in the atelier, and north-facing light. The skylight in Charles's studio did have northern light, and Charles, in these Carmel years, did don a smock that Alice sewed for him. His page-boy haircut was allowed to grow long. The concept of the studio must have been with him for many years. As a young man he had visited artistic salons in

Boston. During his Pasadena years, the southern California home of the historian Charles Fletcher Lummis was notorious for its bohemian gatherings of all the famous artistic types, from John Muir to Sarah Bernhardt. Surely it all held great attraction for Charles as the center of a thoughtful community. 🍃 The Greenes were very much a part of artistic Carmel. They appeared in local theater productions, and his studio was used for concerts, an exhibition and sale of oriental carpets, political gatherings, poetry readings, lectures, and parties where, his daughter-in-law remembers, "coffee and little cakes" were served by Alice. His daughter Anne would spend hours here every day practicing on the Steinway grand while Charles read or did his work. It was also a place where Charles could meditate when alone or, when with a select group of friends, study the writings of the Russian mystic Gurdjieff.

In his studio, more than anywhere else, the presence of Charles Greene can be felt. His hand is everywhere. The massive teak front door, leading to an anteroom, was carved by him with a pattern of fruit-bearing vines growing upward from pots. On other doors are places where Charles started but never finished carving a geometrically stylized floral pattern; pencil and chalk marks remain on the uncarved portion, showing how he was planning to continue. In woodblocks he carved shapes to be used, with the help of the children, to stamp impressions in the soft plaster. His daughter Alice helped him carve the long, heavy beams that stretch across the ceiling. ❧ The construction was not costly for the retired architect. The bricks came cheap, salvaged from an old hotel in Carmel that had been torn down. His sons helped him gather them, tote them home, and clean them by hand. The front door was given to him along with oak for the floors by a San Francisco lumber company as thanks for all the business he had done with them. The redwood beams were from a nearby canyon. Charles never had the roof tiled or gutters installed, probably because he could not afford it. ❧ The floors were covered with oriental carpets, Chinese furniture was situated around the room, and a small Buddhist statue of Jizo was placed in a small arched niche above the fireplace. Some of his oil paintings were stacked inside, along with a three-panel teak folding screen that he had carved himself for a client who had rejected it (no doubt because of the cost) and a massive bookcase carved with gentle, undulating patterns.

Although Charles had built a simple frame cottage for his family, the studio, built later, was where he spent most of the remaining days of his life. He often had his meals here, sometimes even sleeping within its peaceful confines. A gentle light pervades the room today, softened by fabric covering the north-facing skylight.

223

With the help of his daughter Alice, Charles himself carved the large beams that stretch across the ceiling in patterns inspired by the ocean (top and above). Some of the work remains unfinished, including teak doors meant to be carved (right), which separate the studio's main room from the small anteroom facing the street.

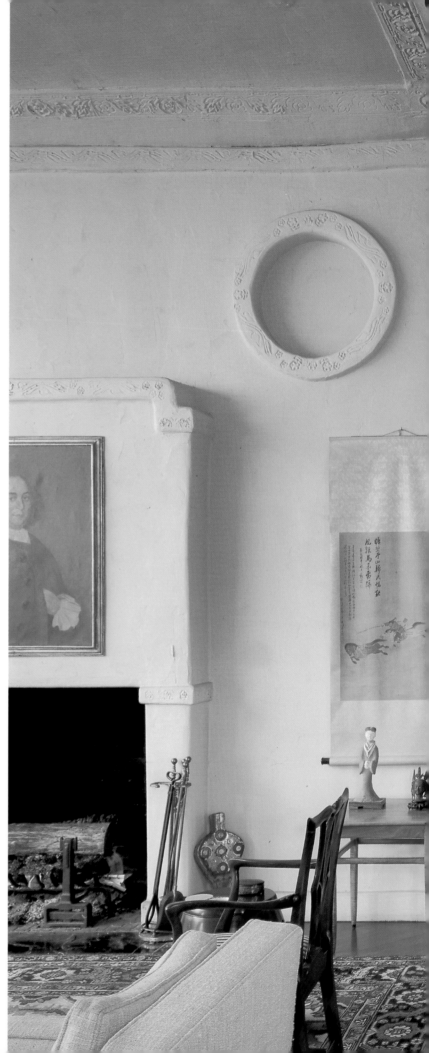

Charles lived here longer than anywhere else. He retreated into the studio's solitude, pondering his Buddhist writings, meditating, carving bits of wood. When the architectural historian Clay Lancaster visited the aging architect in 1954, he felt as though he had been "transported to Never-Never land." Charles was "a tiny old man, very much stooped over, with long strands of white silk hair falling down to his shoulders." Lancaster realized that Charles had so withdrawn into his Buddhism that he had no great concern for "answering factual questions." ❧ The house that Charles built for his family is gone now. It was a simple, board-and-batten structure, simpler than anything he had ever built for Greene and Greene's clients. The interior walls were never finished, the electrical wires were strung along the bare studs. His family called it "the Shack." After Charles and Alice had died, a son demolished it to make room to add bedrooms and a kitchen to the studio. The roof was finally finished, using the same kind of tiles that Charles had chosen for the James House, carefully laid by the original roofer. ❧ Not everything remains within the studio as it was when Charles was alive, yet one still feels his spirit here. Light filtered through the curtains of the skylight casts a gentle glow over the room. Bookcases still contain rows of books he used to hold and ponder. Patterns and images are carved and half-carved in the woodwork. There is a feeling of work done and still to be done in this room held so precious by its architect.

Decorative patterns surrounding a wooden door and edging the ceiling (opposite) were made by Charles with the help of his children. He carved small woodblock stamps that they would press into the wet plaster to leave an impression. A bookcase Charles built for the studio (right) still holds the books he loved to read.

CHRONOLOGY

1868

Charles Sumner Greene born October 12 in Cincinnati

1870

Henry Mather Greene born January 23 in Cincinnati

1887–88

Charles and Henry are graduated
from the Manual Training School in St. Louis

1891

The brothers complete a partial course
in a special two-year architecture program at MIT

1891–93

Charles and Henry serve apprenticeships
in Boston architecture firms

1893

The new architects arrive in Pasadena in September

1897

Greene and Greene moves into the Kinney-Kendall Building
in Pasadena, designed by the firm and built the previous year

1899

Henry marries Emeline Augusta Dart

1901

Charles marries Alice Gordon White and honeymoons
in England, beginning his own home when he returns

Greene and Greene opens a Los Angeles office

1902

Culbertson House designed

1903

Bandini and Van Rossem Houses designed

First alterations done on the Duncan House

Charles's drawings of the Darling House published
in *Academy Architecture* in London

1904

Reeve House designed

Whitridge House designed for Henry's mother-in-law;
Henry and his family move back to Pasadena
from Los Angeles to live with her

Camp, Garfield, and Tichenor Houses designed

1905

Robinson, Brandt-Serrurier, and Libby Houses designed

1906

DeForest and Bolton Houses designed

Extensive additional alterations done on the Duncan House
for Theodore Irwin

Extensive work done on the Van Rossem House
for James Neill

First consequential national article on Greene and Greene
appears in *Architectural Record* in October

1907

Ford, Blacker, and Spinks Houses designed

1908

Gamble House designed

1909

Pratt, Crow, Thorsen, and Anthony Houses designed

Charles shows C. R. Ashbee the firm's work in Pasadena

Charles takes his family to England in April
and returns in November

1911

Culbertson Sisters and Fleishhacker Houses designed

1912

The last major article on the Greenes
appears in the August issue of *The Craftsman*

1913

Ware and Ladd Houses designed

1916
Charles moves with his family to Carmel

1918
James House is begun by Charles working alone

1922
Greene and Greene is dissolved
and Henry reorganizes under his name alone

1923
Charles builds a studio next to his home in Carmel

1927
Charles designs the water garden for the Fleishhacker estate

1939
Charles adds a library to the James House

1948
Southern California Chapter, American Institute of Architects,
honors the brothers with a certificate of merit

1952
American Institute of Architects recognizes Greene and Greene
for its contribution "to the design of the American home"

1954
Henry dies October 2 in Pasadena

1957
Charles dies June 11 in Carmel

1960
Charles's family donates drawings, photographs, and
memorabilia to the Documents Collection, College of
Environmental Design, University of California at Berkeley

1966
Gamble House opens September 25 as a house museum
honoring the work of Greene and Greene

The transition from the inner world of the Duncan-Irwin House
to the natural world outside flows gently from spaces such as the
second-story porch, with its broad overhanging roof. The terraced entry below leads to the porte cochere over the driveway.

EXISTING GREENE & GREENE BUILDINGS

1894

Briener House (John Briener), 740 North Mar Vista;
moved from 826 East Colorado Street

1895

Covelle House (Conrad A. Covelle),
920 Seco Street (with alterations)

Eason House (Robert Eason), 448 North Summit Avenue

Eason House (Willis Eason), 442 North Summit Avenue

1896

Kinney-Kendall Building, 65 East Colorado Street
(with major alterations)

1897

Longley House (Howard Longley), 1005 Buena Vista Street,
South Pasadena (with additions and alterations)

McLean House (Elizabeth McLean),
450 North Raymond Avenue

1898

Hollister House (Charles W. Hollister), 310 Bellefontaine Street

Swan House (Frances Swan),
2162 North Holliston Avenue;
moved from 515 East Colorado Street (with alterations)

1901

Greene House (Charles Sumner Greene), 368 Arroyo Terrace

1902

Barker House (George H. Barker), 505 South Grand Avenue
(half demolished, half remodeled)

Culbertson House (James Culbertson),
235 North Grand Avenue (remodeled)

Dowling House (Frank M. Dowling), 570 North Raymond Avenue

1903

Black House (Emma Black), 210 South Madison Avenue
(with alterations)

Duncan-Irwin House (Katherine Duncan, Theodore Irwin),
240 North Grand Avenue (with alterations and additions
to existing house, plus additions and alterations in 1906)

Sanborn House (Samuel P. Sanborn), 65 North Catalina Avenue;
moved from 999 East Colorado Street

Darling House (Mary Reeve Darling),
807 North College Avenue, Claremont

Rowland House (Dr. Francis F. Rowland), 225 State Street;
moved from 55 South Marengo Avenue (with alterations)

Van Rossem-Neill House (Josephine van Rossem,
James W. Neill), 400 Arroyo Terrace (with alterations in 1906)

White Sisters House (Violet, Jane, and Martha White),
370 Arroyo Terrace (with alterations)

1904

Reeve House (Jennie A. Reeve), 4260 Country Club Drive,
Long Beach; moved from 306 Cedar Avenue (with additions)

Camp House (Edgar Camp),
327 Sierra Woods Drive, Sierra Madre (with additions)

Merwin House (Alexander Merwin), 267 State Street

Van Rossem House (Josephine van Rossem),
210 North Grand Avenue

White House (Kate White), 1036 Brent Avenue, South Pasadena
(with additions and alterations)

Garfield House (Mrs. James A. Garfield), 1001 Buena Vista Street,
South Pasadena (with additions)

Tichenor House (Adelaide M. Tichenor),
852 East Ocean Boulevard, Long Beach (with major alterations)

Reeve House (Jennie A. Reeve), 1265 Loma Vista Drive

1905

Halsted House (S. Hazard Halsted), 90 North Grand Avenue

Robinson House (Henry M. Robinson), 195 South Grand Avenue

Bowen House (William A. Bowen),
443 East Calaveras Street, Altadena (with additions)

Willet House (Charles J. Willet),
424 Arroyo Terrace (with alterations)

Brandt-Serrurier House (A. C. Brandt, Iwan Serrurier),
1086 Mariposa Street, Altadena (with alterations)

Wheeler House (Lucy E. Wheeler),
2175 Cambridge Street, Los Angeles (with alterations)

1906

Reeve House (Jennie A. Reeve),
197 North Mountain Trail, Sierra Madre

Phillips House (John B. Phillips),
459 Bellefontaine Street (with alterations)

Pitcairn House (Robert Pitcairn Jr.),
289 West State Street (with alterations)

Bentz House (John C. Bentz), 657 Prospect Boulevard

DeForest House (Caroline S. DeForest),
530 West California Street

Cole House (John A. Cole),
2 Westmoreland Place (with major alterations)

Hawks House (F. W. Hawks), 408 Arroyo Terrace

Bolton House (Dr. William T. Bolton),
370 Del Mar Street (with alterations)

1907

Ford House (Freeman Ford),
215 South Grand Avenue (with additions and alterations)

Blacker House (Robert R. Blacker), 1177 Hillcrest Avenue

Ranney House (Mary Ranney),
440 Arroyo Terrace (with additions)

Spinks House (William Ward Spinks),
1344 Hillcrest Avenue (built in 1909)

1908

Gamble House (David B. Gamble), 4 Westmoreland Place

1909

Pratt House (Charles M. Pratt), 1330 North Foothill Road, Ojai

Crow-Crocker House (Dr. S. S. Crow, Edward Crocker),
979 South El Molino Avenue

Thorsen House (William R. Thorsen),
2307 Piedmont Avenue, Berkeley

Anthony House (Earle C. Anthony),
910 North Bedford Drive, Beverly Hills;
moved from 666 South Berendo Street, Los Angeles

1910

Smith House (Ernest W. Smith), 272 South Los Robles Avenue

Merrill House (Sam L. Merrill), 1285 Summit Avenue

1911

Huston House (Joseph K. Huston), 605 North Marengo Avenue

Henry W. Longfellow Elementary School,
1065 East Washington Street (with alterations)

Bentz House (Nathan Bentz),
1741 Prospect Avenue, Santa Barbara (with alterations)

Culbertson Sisters House (Cordelia Culbertson),
1188 Hillcrest Avenue

Fleishhacker House (Mortimer Fleishhacker),
Woodside

1912

Parker Apartment House (Earle J. Parker),
527 Union Street (with alterations)

Blacker House (Annie Blacker), 675 South Madison Avenue

1913

Ware House (Henry Ware), 460 Bellefontaine Street

Ladd House (William M. Ladd), 818 North Foothill Road, Ojai

1915

Williams House (Dr. Nathan H. Williams),
1145 Sonoma Drive, Altadena

Greene House (John T. Greene),
3200 H Street, Sacramento (with alterations)

1917

Mundorff House (Howard F. Mundorff),
3753 Balch Street, Fresno

Witbeck House (Charles S. Witbeck),
226 Palisades Avenue, Santa Monica

1918

James House (D. L. James), Route 1, Carmel Highlands

1920

Schevill Studio (Rudolph Schevill), 77 Tamalpais Road, Berkeley

1923

Tolmie House (Robert Tolmie), 250 Scenic Avenue, Piedmont
(with additions) (Charles Greene commission)

Charles Greene Studio (Charles Sumner Greene),
Lincoln Avenue and 13th Street, Carmel (with additions)
(Charles Greene commission)

1924

Gould House (Thomas Gould),
402 Lynn Drive, Ventura (Henry Greene commission)

Savage Duplex (Arthur Savage),
1299–1301 North Marengo Avenue (Henry Greene commission)

Kelley House (Kate Kelley), 2550 Aberdeen Street, Los Angeles
(with additions and alterations) (Henry Greene commission)

1925

Mardian Store (Samuel Z. Mardian),
1517–25 East Washington Street (with major alterations)
(Henry Greene commission)

Thum House (William Thum), 1507 Mountain Street
(with alterations) (Henry Greene commission)

Morrison House (Lloyd Morrison), 1414 Alhambra Road,
South Pasadena (Henry Greene commission)

1929

Howard House (John Langley Howard), 86 Ave Maria Road,
Monterey (with alterations) (Charles Greene commission)

Richardson House (Walter L. Richardson),
27349 Avenue 138, Porterville (Henry Greene commission)

McElwain House (Alan McElwain), 18000 Bull Canyon Road,
Granada Hills (Henry Greene commission)

The years indicated are the design dates.
Where no city is given, the location is Pasadena.

LOST GREENE & GREENE BUILDINGS

Like the Bandini House of 1903, the residence the Greenes designed a year later for the Charles W. Hollister family enclosed a courtyard on three sides. Alive with green grass and gurgling water from the fountain, this outdoor oasis became an extension of the living space— a perfect solution for California's climate. The Bandini and Hollister Houses are among many Greene and Greene designs now demolished.

1894

Flynn House (Martha Flynn), 96 North El Molino Avenue

Pasadena Security Investment Company,
100 South El Molino Avenue

Pasadena Security Investment Company No. 3,
80 South Madison Avenue

1895

Rigg House (Dr. Thomas J. Rigg), 49 South Madison Avenue

Crump House (Edward S. Crump), 716 Union Street

Eldred House (Charles Eldred), 881 North Raymond Avenue

1896

Allen House (Robert Allen), 325 South Euclid Avenue

Miller House (Rollin Miller), 292 Bellefontaine Street

Gartzman House (Charlotte Gartzman),
54 North Madison Avenue

Barker House (George H. Barker), address unknown, Altadena

Hosmer House (Edward B. Hosmer),
229 South Orange Grove Boulevard

1897

Neumeister House (John Neumeister), 415 South Lake Avenue

Gordon House (Theodore P. Gordon),
820 North Los Robles Avenue

Hull House and Office (Dr. George S. Hull),
36–46 North Los Robles Avenue

1898

Fay House (Winthrop Fay), 71 South Euclid Avenue

Roberts House (Dr. W. Hume Roberts), 29 North Euclid Avenue

Tompkins House (William B. Tompkins),
San Rafael Avenue near Nithsdale Road

Bennett House (Mary A. Bennett), 104 North Los Robles Avenue

1899

Smith House (J. M. Smith), 125 Terrace Drive

Sanborn House (Samuel F. Sanborn), 695 East Colorado Street

1900

Milnor House (Mary R. Milnor), 385 South Euclid Avenue

Bolton House (Dr. William T. Bolton),
101 North Los Robles Avenue

Pasadena Ice Company, west side of South Broadway

Smith House (John M. Smith), 370 West Colorado Street

1901

Phillips House (Metilde Phillips), 151 South Fair Oaks Avenue

Bentz Building (John C. Bentz), 49–55 South Raymond Avenue

Hansen House (Lorenz P. Hansen), 968 San Pasqual Street

Hansen House (Lorenz P. Hansen), 1000 San Pasqual Street

Swett House (H. Sybil Swett), 343 Waverly Drive

Brown House (Benjamin C. Brown),
120 North El Molino Avenue

Ker House (James F. Ker), 126 North Madison Avenue

1902

All Saints Episcopal Church Rectory, 132 North Euclid Avenue

King House (Mary King), address unknown

Bolton House (Dr. William T. Bolton), 284 Madison Avenue

Rasey Rooming House (Rose J. Rasey), 158 North Euclid Avenue

1903

Lund House (Dr. George Lund),
1227 Maryland Street, Los Angeles

Auten House (Phillip Auten), 119 North Madison Avenue

Martin Studio Apartments (F. J. Martin),
225 North Madison Avenue

Claypole House (Dr. Edith J. Claypole), 50 South Grand Avenue

Bandini House (Arturo Bandini), 1149 San Pasqual Street

1904

Hollister House (Charles W. Hollister), west side of Cahuenga
Boulevard, north of Hollywood Boulevard, Hollywood

Whitridge House (Charlotte Whitridge, Henry's mother-in-law),
146 Bellefontaine Street

Abbott House (George E. Abbott), 165 North Los Robles Avenue

Green House (Roger Henry Carleton Green),
1919 Robson Street, Vancouver, British Columbia

Brandt House (A. C. Brandt), 394 North Garfield Avenue

1905

Libbey House (Dr. Arthur A. Libbey),
665 South Orange Grove Boulevard

Porter House (L. G. and Marion Porter),
1957 Hobart Boulevard, Los Angeles

Serrurier House (Iwan Serrurier), 805 East California Street

1906

Pasadena Ice Company, east side of South Broadway

Pomona Valley Ice Company, 1163 East Second Street, Pomona

1908

Silent House (Charles K. Silent),
Palm Drive and Grand Avenue, Glendora

Lawless House (William J. Lawless),
585 Sierra Madre Boulevard, Sierra Madre

1911

Brown House (Charles G. Brown), 665 North Marengo Avenue

1912

Kew House (Michael Kew), 3224 Sixth Avenue, San Diego

1914

Engleman House (Dr. Rosa Engleman), 1235 San Pasqual Street

1915

Hamlin House (William Hamlin),
150 South Orange Grove Boulevard

1920

Charles Greene House (Charles Sumner Greene),
Lincoln Avenue and 13th Street, Carmel

1921

Greene House (Dr. Thomas Sumner Greene
and Lelia Mather Greene, Charles and Henry's parents),
Monteverde Avenue at 13th Street, Carmel

233

1925

Greene House (Bettie Greene),
address unknown, Carmel (Charles Greene commission)

Student Club House, California Institute of Technology,
1201 East California Street (Henry Greene commission)

1926

Bates House (Alice Greene Bates),
address unknown, Lakeport (Charles Greene commission)

Saunders House (Mrs. James E. Saunders),
130 Bellefontaine Street (Henry Greene commission)

1929

Strasburg House (Mrs. Edward Strasburg),
225 West Adams Park Drive, Covina (Henry Greene commission)

The years indicated are the design dates.
Where no city is given, the location was Pasadena.

GENERAL: The three primary archives of materials relating to Charles and Henry Greene and their work are held at the Documents Collection of the College of Environmental Design Library, University of California, Berkeley; the Avery Library, Columbia University, New York City; and the Greene and Greene Library at the Huntington Library, San Marino, California, which serves as the research archives of the Gamble House–University of Southern California.

Beyond books and articles listed in Further Reading, I have relied on interviews conducted over the past seven years with descendants of Charles and Henry Greene as well as with current owners of houses designed by Greene and Greene, in addition to various other sources. Of great use was "Charles Sumner Greene and Henry Mather Greene, Architects: An Annotated Bibliography," by Margaret Meriwether (1993). In addition, several good graduate theses provide valuable insights about the Greenes, specifically Stuart Bailey's "The Gamble House, 1908: An Analytical Description of a Residence in Pasadena, California, In View of Some of the Influences Affecting Its Design" (master's thesis, Claremont Graduate School, 1954); John Caldwell's "A Graphic and Historical Inquiry into the Furniture of Charles and Henry Greene" (master's thesis, Los Angeles State College of Applied Arts and Sciences, 1964); Barbara Ann Francis's "The Boston Roots of Greene and Greene" (master's thesis, Tufts University, 1987); and Travis Culwell's "The Spirituality of Charles Sumner Greene" (master's thesis, University of California, Berkeley, 1995).

Specific sources follow.

THE GREENE AND GREENE STYLE, Page 28: "there are three ... " Charles Greene, "Bungalows," *The Western Architect* 12 (July 1908): 3. CHARLES GREENE HOUSE, Page 55: "From its high position ... " and "Arroyo Terrace is not ... " Charles Greene, "Bungalows," *The Western Architect* 12 (July 1908): 5. "the needed privacy ... " and "from the dust ... " "Bungalows," 4. CULBERTSON HOUSE, Page 59: "the furniture and ... " Una Nixson Hopkins, "A Study for Home-Builders," *Good Housekeeping* 45 (March 1906): 262. For general information about the Culbertson House, see "1897 House Remodeled," *Sunset* 53 (September 1955): 52–53; "A Fine Old House Remodeled with Respect," *House and Home* 9 (March 1956): 180–86; "A Great Old House Lives On," *House Beautiful* 105 (February 1962): 118–25; other information came from the author's interview with Whitney Smith. DARLING HOUSE, Page 67: "when the sliding doors ... " and "my own private sanctum ... " Kenneth G. Darling, *My Early Life in California and My First American and European Tours (1890–1908)* (n.p., n.d.). At Honnold Library, Claremont Colleges, Rare Book Room, 15. "evenings spent in intimate ... " *My Early Life*, 16. "Here I listened to ... " *My Early Life*, 17. I am grateful to David Alexander for providing relevant passages. See also *Academy Architecture*, pt. 2, vol. 23 (1903). CAMP HOUSE, Page 68: "who are responsible for ... " "A Mountain Bungalow Whose Appearance of Crude Construction Is the Result of Skillful Design," *The Craftsman* 17 (November 1909): 329. "in one respect ... " Edgar Camp, "E. W. Camp Memorandum," 40. Courtesy of Ann Nourse. "in the evenings we ... " "E. W. Camp Memorandum," 42. Page 71: For the story of the Bandini House, see Jean Murray Bangs, "Greene and Greene: The American House Owes Simplicity and Clarity to Two Almost-Forgotten Brothers Who Showed Us How to Build with Wood," *Architectural Forum* 89 (October 1948): 85. ROBINSON HOUSE, Page 76: "simple but spacious ... " Rockwell Hereford, *A Whole Man and a Half Century* (Pacific Grove, Calif.: The Boxwood Press, 1985), 45. "was placed on the western ... " Henry Mather Greene, "The Use of Orange

Trees in Formal Gardens," *California Southland* (April 1919): 8. BENTZ HOUSE, Pages 86–89: All quotations are from the author's 1992 interviews with Helen Bentz Witherbee. BOLTON HOUSE, Page 102: "better described as a ... " Ken Ross, "Resurrecting the Bolton House," *Fine Homebuilding* 17 (October–November 1983): 29. VAN ROSSEM–NEILL HOUSE, Page 122: "With its field stones ... " Charles Greene, "Bungalows," *Western Architect* 12 (July 1908): 5. BLACKER HOUSE, Page 126: "the spell of Japan ... " Robert Winter, "American Sheaves from 'C. R. A.,'" *Journal of the Society of Architectural Historians* 30 (December 1971): 321. Page 128: "the Japanese Garden ... " A. W. Alley, "A House in Japanese Style," *House Beautiful* 25 (March 1909): 76. For general information about the Blacker House, see Tim Gregory, "1177 Hillcrest Avenue, Pasadena: The Blacker House" (1993). RANNEY HOUSE, Page 137: "rustic", "a suggestion of old Swiss ... ", "weathered redwood ... ", "rough redwood ... ", "the absolute simplicity ... ", and "the woodwork is ... " Helen Lukens Gaut, "California Bungalows Costing One Thousand Dollars Upwards," *American Homes and Gardens* 7 (March 1910): 94. "People of Pasadena called my first ... " Documents Collection, College of Environmental Design Library, University of California, Berkeley (hereafter CED Archives). SPINKS HOUSE, Page 154: "a quiet, dreamy ... " Robert Winter, "American Sheaves from 'C. R. A.,'" *Journal of the Society of Architectural Historians* 30 (December 1971): 322. THORSEN HOUSE, Pages 170–77: For information on William Thorsen and the Thorsen House, I am indebted to Robert Judson Clark. ANTHONY HOUSE, Page 178: "Charles Sumner Greene ... " *Pasadena News*, 24 December 1909: 9. CULBERTSON SISTERS HOUSE, Page 186: "somewhat definite in the cost ... " and "Speaking of estimates ... " CED Archives. FLEISHHACKER HOUSE, Page 193: "Green Greene" and "Pink Greene." Anne Bloomfield, "The Evolution of a Landscape: Charles Sumner Greene's Designs for Green Gables," *Journal of the Society of Architectural Historians* 47 (September 1988): 233. Page 194: "sit on the little hill ... " "Evolution of a Landscape," 237. For general information about the Fleishhacker House, see David Streatfield, "Echoes of England and Italy 'On the Edge of the World': Green Gables and Charles Greene," *Journal of Garden History* 2 (October–December 1982): 377–98. I am indebted to Robert Judson Clark for this information. JAMES HOUSE, Page 208: "to ponder life ... ", "Is there more ... ", "Is there anything ... ", "I broke my vow ... ", and "I am everything ... " CED Archives. "was passionate about ... " Dan James's interview with Randell Makinson. I am grateful to Mr. Makinson for sharing this information. Dan James's biographical notes about his family are in the Greene and Greene Library. The information about Elizabeth Gordon is from the author's interviews with Gordon and Bunny Pratt. See also "The Undiscovered Beauty of Our Recent Past," *House Beautiful* 99 (January 1957): 48–53; and "Discovering Our Recent Past," *House Beautiful* 99 (December 1957): 152–63. For the English connection, see Edward R. Bosley, "Greene and Greene: The British Connection," *The Tabby* 1, no. 3 (July–August 1997): 6–21. CHARLES GREENE STUDIO, Page 220: "coffee and little cakes." Betty Patchin Greene, "Historic Houses: Charles Greene. The Arts and Crafts Architect's Studio in Carmel," *Architectural Digest* 46 (May 1989): 104. Page 227: "transported to ... " and "a tiny old ... " Clay Lancaster, "My Interviews with Greene and Greene," *Journal of the American Institute of Architects* 28 (July 1957): 203. "answering factual ... " "My Interviews with Greene and Greene," 204. "the Shack." Author's interview with Anne Roberts. For information about Charles Greene's studio, I am grateful for interviews with Thomas and Betty Greene, Anne Roberts, and Clay Lancaster.

ACKNOWLEDGMENTS

I am in debt to Edward R. Bosley, Robert Judson Clark, Randell Makinson, and Robert Winter for so generously sharing of their researches. I am grateful to the staffs of the archives at the Documents Collection of the College of Environmental Design Library, University of California, Berkeley; the Avery Library, Columbia University, New York City; and the Greene and Greene Library, the research archives of the Gamble House—University of Southern California, at the Huntington Library, San Marino, for their time and helpfulness. The staff and docents of the Gamble House have been a constant source of support, encouragement, and good cheer, especially Lee Sanders, Bobbi Mapstone, Judi Benda, Kathy LaShure, and Everardo Farias.

The probing, inquisitive work of Janet Brown Becker, Edward S. Cooke, James Ipekjian, Karen Sinsheimer, Janaan Strand, and Richard Guy Wilson all provided the foundation on which I and others who follow must endeavor to build on. I thank Astrid Ellersieck for her invaluable help in contacting current owners of Greene and Greene houses.

Through my many years of research, the descendants of Charles and Henry Greene not only have been a valuable historical resource but also have given me a sense of who the two brothers were as people. I give thanks especially to Alice Cory, Nancy Glass, Bettie Greene, Isabelle Greene, Ruth Greene, Thomas and Betty Greene, Thomas Casey Greene, Virginia Hales, Isabelle McElwain, Jane Petersen, and the late Nathaniel Patrickson Greene, Philip Greene, and Anne Roberts.

Many people welcomed me into their homes. They understand that where they live is more than just a home, that the walls that surround them are imbued with both history and artistic genius. For entry to their worlds of artistry and history, I thank David and Catherine Alexander, Barbara Babcock, James Benjamin, Bill Bensen, David and Judy Brown, Anthony Bruce, George and Marilyn Brumder, Ann and Andre Chaves, Andrew Chute, Leslie Dixon, John and Anne Dullaghan, Linda and David Duncan, Mortimer Fleishhacker III, Terry Geiser, Peter Gordon, Jacque Heebner, Charles and Katie Hubey, Jan and Wally Hurff, Dan and Ann Hyde, Nancy and Dennis Kailey, Harvey and Ellen Knell, Mark and Ann LaSalle, Chris Lee, Isak Lindenauer, Julia Lyman, Janet Mark, Delany and Bob Marron, Leon Max, Louise Mills, Bill and Jennifer Moses, Dave Munro, Robert and Ruth Peck, Greg Porter, Bunny Pratt, Margine Remund, Thomas and Nancy Rietze, Joe Ritchie, Tom Ropelowski, David Salazar, Susan Schevill, Bill Searle, Whitney Smith, Zachery and Denise Snyder, David Streatfield, Kathleen Thorne-Thomsen, Rick Travers, Steve and Mary Ann Voorhees, Martin Weil, Robert and Glen Whitson, and Kevin Wiems, as well as Sigma Phi Fraternity and Westridge School.

I give special thanks to Ann and Andre Chaves for sharing both food and wisdom with me during my many stays in their home, to Harvey and Ellen Knell for giving me contemplative time alone in what the Greenes counted as their masterpiece, to George and Vicky Kastner for their understanding and friendship, and to my children for their patience during the months I withdrew to work on this book. The work accomplished here I dedicate to the two women who have made me what I am: my mother, Anna Sue Borum Smith (1918–97), and my wife, Yoshiko Yamamoto.

Bruce Smith

235

FURTHER READING

Bosley, Edward R. *Gamble House: Greene and Greene*. London: Phaidon Press, 1992.

——————. "Greene and Greene: The British Connection." *The Tabby: A Chronicle of the Arts and Crafts Movement* 1, no. 3 (July–August 1997): 6–21.

——————. "Greene and Greene: An Overview of the Past Hundred Years. An Introduction to the Centennial Lecture Series." In *Centennial Lectures: Greene and Greene, 1894–1994*. Pasadena: Friends of the Gamble House, 1994.

Calistro, Paddy, and Betty Goodwin. "Ranney House." In *L.A. Inside Out: The Architecture and Interiors of America's Most Colorful City*. New York: Viking Studio, Penguin, 1992.

Cooke, Edward S., Jr. "Charles Sumner Greene and Henry Mather Greene." In *"The Art That Is Life": The Arts and Crafts Movement in America, 1875–1920*, edited by Wendy Kaplan. Museum of Fine Arts, Boston. Boston: Little, Brown, 1987.

——————. "Scandinavian Modern Furniture in the Arts and Crafts Period: The Collaboration of the Greenes and the Halls." In *American Furniture, 1993*, edited by Luke Beckerdite. Hanover and London: Chipstone Foundation, 1993.

Current, William R. and Karen. *Greene and Greene: Architects in the Residential Style*. Fort Worth, Tex.: Amon Carter Museum of Western Art, 1974.

Fine Homebuilding Great Houses: Craftsman-Style Houses. Newtown, Conn.: Taunton Press, 1991. James and Bolton Houses.

Gale, Iain, and Richard Bryant. "The Gamble House." In *Living Museums*. Boston: Bulfinch Press, Little, Brown, 1993.

Germany, Lisa. *Harwell Hamilton Harris*. Austin: University of Texas Press, 1991. Rediscovery and influence of the Greenes' work.

Greene and Greene Interiors, '83: The Duncan-Irwin House Exhibition and Tours. Introduction by Randell Makinson; text by Janeen Marrin. Exhibition catalogue. Pasadena: Gamble House, University of Southern California, 1983.

Hales, Virginia Dart Greene. *The Memoirs of Henry Dart Greene and Ruth Elisabeth Haight Greene*. Vol. 1. La Jolla, Calif.: Virginia Dart Greene Hales, 1996.

Hawley, Henry. "An Italianate Garden by Greene and Greene." *Journal of Decorative and Propaganda Arts*, no. 2 (summer–fall 1986): 32–44. Culbertson Sisters House.

Jordy, William H. "Craftsmanship as Structural Elaboration: Charles and Henry Greene's Gamble House." In *American Buildings and Their Architects*. Vol. 4, *Progressive and Academic Ideals at the Turn of the Twentieth Century*. New York: Oxford University Press, 1972.

Kazor, Virginia, ed. *Greene and Greene: The Architecture and Related Designs of Charles Sumner Greene and Henry Mather Greene, 1894–1934*. Los Angeles: Los Angeles Municipal Arts Department and University of Southern California, 1977.

Lancaster, Clay. *The American Bungalow*. New York: Abbeville Press, 1985.

——————. *The Japanese Influence in America*. New York: Walton H. Rawls, 1963.

——————. "My Interviews with Greene and Greene." *AIA Journal*, July 1957, 202–6.

——————. "Some Sources of Greene and Greene." *AIA Journal*, August 1960, 39–46.

Last of the Ultimate Bungalows: The William R. Thorsen House of Greene and Greene. Exhibition catalogue. Pasadena: Gamble House, University of Southern California, 1996.

Makinson, Randell L. "Charles and Henry Greene." In *Toward a Simpler Way of Life: The Arts and Crafts Architects of California*, edited by Robert Winter. Berkeley: University of California Press, 1997.

————. "Greene and Greene: The Adelaide Tichenor House." *The Tabby: A Chronicle of the Arts and Crafts Movement* 1, no. 3 (July–August 1997): 22–38.

————. *Greene and Greene: Architecture as a Fine Art.* Salt Lake City: Peregrine Smith, 1977.

————. *Greene and Greene: Furniture and Related Designs.* Salt Lake City: Peregrine Smith, 1979.

————. "Greene and Greene: The Gamble House" and "An Academic Paper: The Gamble House." *Prairie School Review* 5, no. 4 (1968): 5–26.

————. *A Guide to the Work of Greene and Greene.* Salt Lake City: Peregrine Smith, 1974.

Marks, Alan. "Greene and Greene: A Study in Functional Design." *Fine Woodworking* 12 (September 1978): 40–45.

McAlester, Virginia and Lee. "Gamble House." In *Great American Houses and Their Architectural Styles.* New York: Abbeville Press, 1994.

McCoy, Esther. "The California House: How It Started." *Los Angeles Times Home Magazine,* July 19, 1953, 13–17.

————. *Five California Architects.* New York: Reinhold, 1960.

————. "Notes on Greene and Greene." *Arts and Architecture,* July 1953, 27.

————. *Roots of California Contemporary Architecture.* Exhibition catalogue. Los Angeles: Los Angeles Art Commission and Municipal Art Department, 1956.

————. "Roots of California Contemporary Architecture." *Arts and Architecture,* September 1956, 36–59.

————. "Seven Pioneers Who Showed the Way." *Los Angeles Times Home Magazine,* September 9, 1956, 13–17.

Oak Knoll, 1910. Pasadena: Friends of the Gamble House, 1995. Culbertson Sisters and Spinks Houses and Blacker garage and keeper's cottage.

Page, Marian. "The Greene Brothers." In *Furniture Designed by Architects.* New York: Whitney Library of Design, 1980.

Smith, Bruce. "Historical Remembrance." *The Tabby: A Chronicle of the Arts and Crafts Movement* 1, no. 3 (July–August 1997): 2–5.

Stickley, Gustav. *Craftsman Homes: Architecture and Furnishings of the American Arts and Crafts Movement.* 1909. Reprint, New York: Dover Publications, 1979.

————. "A Mountain Bungalow. . . . " In *Craftsman Bungalows: 59 Homes from "The Craftsman."* 1903–16. Reprint, with an introduction by Alan Weissman, New York: Dover Publications, 1988. Camp House.

————. ed. "California's Contribution to a National Architecture: Its Significance and Beauty as Shown in the Work of Greene and Greene, Architects." In *The Craftsman: An Anthology,* edited by Barry Sanders. Salt Lake City: Peregrine Smith, 1978.

Strand, Janann. *A Greene and Greene Guide.* Pasadena: Grant Dahlstrom, Castle Press, 1974.

Streatfield, David C. "Arts and Crafts Gardens." In *California Gardens: Creating a New Eden.* New York: Abbeville Press, 1994.

————. "Echoes of England and Italy 'On the Edge of the World': Green Gables and Charles Greene." *Journal of Garden History* 2, no. 4 (October–December 1982): 377–98.

Thomas, Jeanette A. *Images of the Gamble House: Masterwork of Greene and Greene.* Pasadena: Gamble House, University of Southern California, 1989.

INDEX

239